Imagining The Gospels

*Cycle B Sermons for Lent & Easter
Based on the Gospel Texts*

Reverend Timothy W. Ayers

CSS Publishing Company, Inc.
Lima, Ohio

IMAGINING THE GOSPELS
CYCLE B SERMONS FOR LENT AND EASTER
BASED ON GOSPEL TEXTS

FIRST EDITION
Copyright © 2017
by CSS Publishing Co., Inc.

Published by CSS Publishing Company, Inc., Lima, Ohio 45807. All rights reserved. No part of this publication may be reproduced in any manner whatsoever without the prior permission of the publisher, except in the case of brief quotations embodied in critical articles and reviews. Inquiries should be addressed to: CSS Publishing Company, Inc., Permissions Department, 5450 N. Dixie Highway, Lima, Ohio 45807.

Library of Congress Cataloging-in-Publication Data
Names: Ayers, T. W. (Timothy Wayne), 1950- author.
Title: Imaging the Gospels : Gospel sermons for Lent & Easter Cycle B based on the Gospel texts / Reverend Timothy W. Ayers.
Description: FIRST EDITION. | Lima, Ohio : CSS Publishing Company, Inc., 2017. | Includes bibliographical references and index.
Identifiers: LCCN 2017019837 (print) | LCCN 2017027980 (ebook) | ISBN 9780788029110 (eBook) | ISBN 0788029118 (eBook) | ISBN 9780788029103 (pbk.: alk. paper) | ISBN 078802910X (pbk. : alk. paper)
Subjects: LCSH: Bible. Gospels--Sermons. | Lenten sermons. | Eastertide--Sermons. | Church year sermons. | Common lectionary (1992). Year B.
Classification: LCC BS2555.54 (ebook) | LCC BS2555.54 .A94 2017 (print) | DDC 252/.62--dc23
For more information about CSS Publishing Company resources, visit our website at www.csspub.com, email us at csr@csspub.com, or call (800) 241-4056.

e-book:
ISBN-13: 978-0-7880-2911-0
ISBN-10: 0-7880-2911-8

ISBN-13: 978-0-7880-2910-3
ISBN-10: 0-7880-2910-X   PRINTED IN USA

Dedication

This book is dedicated to all those who sat through my earliest messages and survived. I recognize now that it was their love for Christ and me that kept them in their seats. Bless you for your kindness. It is also dedicated to every pastor that must climb those steps every Sunday morning to stand in front of a congregation seeking to know more about God and about our Savior. It is also dedicated to my family because they support me, no matter what. It is dedicated to Marylee who taught me about lunch box sermons and also to Yvonne who suffered through the early ones. It is dedicated to Jude, a very smart ten-year-old who converses easily on the scripture and the fine art of play; to Lily, who will master all words once she gets by ooombarelala; to Zach and Cam because they have heard me preach many times and still call me Papa with love in their hearts; and to Becca, who spent a lot of time listening to her dad and is now supportive of my son-in-law's great weekly messages. It is dedicated to Chuck, who loves my daughter and preaches the word seriously to his great, loving congregation, as well as to Hollywood Bible Chapel that "developed my gift." Finally, this is dedicated to CSS who believes in me more than I do.

Contents

Foreword   7

Ash Wednesday   9
Matthew 6:1-6, 16-21
Beginning The Lenten Journey

First Sunday in Lent   15
Mark 1:9-15
Tearing The Sky To Get To You

Second Sunday of Lent   19
Mark 8:31-38, Mark 9:2-9
Did I Say That Out Loud?

Third Sunday of Lent   23
John 2:13-22
The Road To The Passover

Fourth Sunday of Lent   31
John 3:14-21
A Nod Of Recognition

Fifth Sunday in Lent   37
John 12:20-33
An Encounter With Jesus

Palm Sunday / Passion Sunday   41
Mark 11:1-11, John 12:12-16
It's Sunday…But Friday's Comin'

Maundy Thursday   49
John 13:1-17, 31b-35
Wash All Of Me

Good Friday 53
John 18:1, 19:42
Get The Picture?

The Resurrection Of Our Lord / Easter Sunday 57
John 20:1-18 or Mark 16:1-8
Profiles In Joy

Easter 2 63
John 20:19-31
I Doubt It!

Easter 3 67
Luke 22:36b-48
Don't Fall

Easter 4 73
John 10:11-18
And That's All I Need To Know

Easter 5 77
John 15:1-8
How Does Your Garden Grow?

Easter 6 83
John 15:9-17
Love Is A Verb

Ascension of the Lord 89
Luke 24:44-53
Your Mission If You Choose To Accept It

Easter 7 95
John 17:6-19
As You Sent Me, Then I Send Them

Foreword

As a pastor who writes his messages while also writing novels, children's books, and short dramas, I found myself working hard to visually create the picture of what was happening in the gospel accounts. Why? These were people listening to Jesus. They would have had emotions about the topics. They would have had little things they recognized when Jesus spoke about lambs, shepherds, and vines. Much like our congregants, there would be nods of recognition toward experiences in their lives. My goal was to get the listener to imagine themselves, with their feelings, their reasons for being in church, and use their cognitive skills, inside the story.

At other times, I sought to take them on a week by week journey through the Easter season. I don't assume they have a relationship with Christ. I don't assume they are vibrant, serving members of the congregation. I only assume that the listener is seeking something they do not have. I was attempting to take them one more step on a journey from week to week.

At times I tried to bring humor to the scene in order to lighten the mood of the listener. The body relaxes when we laugh and that helps us to hear the message. If these sermons have helped you please contact the publisher and let them know.

Ash Wednesday
Matthew 6:1-6, 16-21

Beginning The Lenten Journey

I read of a pastor, who confessedly tells that he is not the neatest person in the world, but discovered his daughter was on the way to becoming an even messier housekeeper than he. His approach was always to come at a problem not only with both self-confession and identification but with a bit of humor. When she came home from school one day, he caught her as she walked in the door and said, "I have bad news and good news. The bad news is that we were broken into today. The good news is that they only ransacked one room, throwing clothes, hangers, books, plates, papers all over the floor. They only ransacked one room—yours."

As a teenager is likely to do, she rolled her eyes and went off to her room to clean it. As a good example, he went to his office to straighten things up as well. In many ways, that is what the Lenten season is about. It is about cleaning up our closets and our rooms. It is forty days of a progressive reevaluation and restructuring. We clean up our closets and rooms in preparation for presenting a clean house, or in the more biblical expression, a clean temple.

If we use that as the basis for understanding this passage and for viewing what we are doing here on this Wednesday then we can begin a very important journey toward a spiritual wholeness. In our gospel reading, Jesus says, "Be careful not to practice your righteousness in front of others." That seems to contradict our actions on Ash Wednesday. We come here and have ashes on our foreheads then head out to dinner, the mall, or to visit friends. Sometimes it is hard to put our practices next to the scriptures and have it make sense, but it does.

Let's imagine this scene. Jesus has called the great multitude of people who were following him to an expansive rise of land near the Sea of Galilee. There was a reason for this. The area, given the right wind, acted like an amplifier for someone speaking. In that mass of people there would be common people of the time: rabbis, religious leaders, Pharisees and Sadducees. His words, deeds, and actions drew people to him. According to the scripture, he drew a multitude of people across socio-economic strati. As the Word of God intended, it struck the hearts of the hearers in extremely personal ways.

To one side of him there would have been a group of fishermen, to another direction a group of merchants, and further back there would have been religious leaders seeking to judge the words and teachings of this young rabbi. They would have been there not for evil reasons, but for the reason that any pastor would listen to the messages of a preacher that was drawing the attention of his own flock. They would have been there to hear and assess. It was their role to protect their sheep.

Jesus used many common and historical teachings of Judaism for that time period. They heard little that they could argue with. The younger rabbis would have turned to their teachers and said things like, his teachings are true, are they not, Rabbi? The old man would pull on his beard, giving an earnest thoughtful look then nod his head slowly up and down. The old rabbi would be waiting for this new teacher to snare himself. Instead, Jesus continued his discourse. He told them the type of person who was blessed. He told them how to respond to the law. He told the people that murder occurs first in the heart.

Then Jesus gave instructions on what the crowd must do to be perfect as God is perfect. As the old saying goes, he went from preaching to meddling in the eyes of the religious leaders. Once he began to strip away the masks, hearts moved closer or further away. Each person would have known what Jesus meant by a mask. They had seen Greek plays in some form. The audience's minds would go back to that strong visual. They would be remembering the actors who wore masks to hide who they were. One man could have played several parts in a play and he would need a mask to differentiate the characters. The actor used a mask to display the emotions attached to his character's lines. Masks hid the true nature of the speaker. With one word, hypocrite, Jesus had created an image for each hearer of a man behind a mask pretending to be something he wasn't. Most people listening would have known who Jesus was talking about. They would have shot quick glances toward the religious leaders in their long robes adorned with bright colors and symbols. The crowd would easily see that Jesus was saying not to display a false piety. Jesus was telling them to not try and impress the person next to you with how righteous or holy you are. That would be very freeing for the average working Joe.

Working Joe would have looked on every religious leader and felt vastly inferior. He would have seen him in the synagogue, parading toward the offering plate, dropping in large bags of money. Working Joe would have seen the Pharisee standing on the corner, praying, lifting his hands to heaven. He saw how the pious acted and it was a good example of what Working Joe wasn't and a good example that Working Joe could never be righteous, like the religious leaders.

When Jesus said, "Don't be a hypocrite," he struck a chord in the hearts of that fisherman, that woman struggling to feed her family and not able to give large sums of money, that simple farmer or that tent maker. But it also struck a chord with the Pharisees and the religious leaders. That young rabbi would have turned to his teacher, his mentor, and whispered, "Is he talking about us? Are we being hypocrites? Am I wearing a mask?"

On the other side of the venerable rabbi, possibly, stood a Pharisee who had been fasting. Everyone knew he was fasting. Everyone knew he was pious because he made sure everyone knew he was fasting and very pious. Jesus possibly set his eyes on the old man when he said that fasting should be done as a private event. Don't look like your fasting. Appear as if you're not because fasting is for your personal approach to a holier life, not for others to see and say, "What a holy man he is."

These religious leaders were storing up their treasures here on earth, literally. None of what they did was lasting before God. None of God's good will was gained by their sacrifices or their suffering. They weren't cleaning their rooms. Instead they were shoving everything into the closet, spraying the room with an air freshener and saying it was all done. Making matters even worse, they were saying for others to do it like them.

In the same way, putting a cross of ashes on your forehead is not cleaning your room. Ashes on your forehead is recognizing that there is a need to start cleaning. Lent is a journey of spiritual renewal. Putting ashes on your forehead should be a sign, not to others, but to the man or woman in the mirror that we are taking the first step. If not it is as hollow as this story that I heard of a boy whose brother took him to get ashes on Ash Wednesday. Instead of going to church they went to McDonald's where the older brother dipped his finger in the ash tray and rubbed ashes on their foreheads.

Or as hollow as the man who lived anything but a righteous life, but would go to church early in the day to get his ashes, then parade around at work so all could see what a righteous man he was. In both cases, they wore the mask of righteousness but never experienced the meaning or the reality that their spiritual journey of renewal was starting at the moment.

Then why do this? Why take a visible and outward sign and display it before the world? That's the answer right there. We do it not for the world to see. We do it not to prove how righteous or religious we are. We do it because we know we are sinners. We do it because we know Jesus is the cure for our sin problem. We do it because we want to look in the mirror and see a man or woman who has made that first conscious step towards the renewing our minds and spirits. We do it to make a difference in our lives, to make a difference in the lives around us. It is a pact with the Lord that reminds us and us only that the journey has begun. Ashes are a wonderful symbol of this because ashes throughout scripture were used to indicate repentance, a change of mind, a change of direction and a change of heart. Ashes are not the end all of why you are here. They are the beginning of your Lenten journey of renewal.

Amen.

First Sunday in Lent
Mark 1:9-15

Tearing The Sky To Get To You

No one in the growing crowd saw anything out of the ordinary. Not even those standing a few feet away from John heard the voice. Not a single person felt the ripping of the air above their heads. Only one person saw it. Only one person heard it. Only one person felt the sky rip apart. Even without witnesses we know the account was absolutely true. We know it occurred because the one who told about it was Jesus, the Son of God, who could not lie. It is the event that began the ministry of Jesus as he started his march to the cross.

The scene began with John the Baptist baptizing people in the River Jordan. John's is a great story, integral to the beginning of Jesus' ministry. John was the forerunner predicted in Malachi 3:1. John was a fulfillment of a prophecy that meant that the kingdom of God was at hand and the Messiah was coming soon. His message was a message of hope. It came from a man who had given up the comforts of the world. He wore a tunic made of woven camel's hair tied at his waist with a leather belt. It was not silky and smooth. It was rough and scratchy. He shed the comforts of the world because the soft and silky materials were for the kings and the apparent leaders of his faith. John's clothes also identified him with Elijah because that also fulfilled an Old Testament prophecy.

John had gone into the wilderness. He existed on a diet of locusts and honey. Locusts or grasshoppers were both a permitted food source for Jews to eat and a tremendous source of protein. They were most populous at certain times of the year and near water sources. Being a baptizer would put him near the water's edge and near his source of food. He sought no human comfort but existed to preach the coming kingdom of God and the coming Messiah.

On this day, as John was baptizing and preaching he noticed a man stepping down to the shore then into the water with him. John had been in the wilderness for a long time. He would not have known his cousin at first glance. He would have heard the story of both his own birth and Jesus' birth. He knew the prophecies. He knew who Jesus was but had not seen him lately. When his cousin reached him in the River Jordan, John said to him and those standing at the shore, "Look, the Lamb of God who takes away the sin of the world! This is the one about whom I said, 'After me comes a man who is greater than I am, because he existed before me.' I did not recognize him, but I came baptizing with water so that he could be revealed to Israel."

John felt that he needed to be baptized by Jesus but for the purpose of identifying with John's ministry, he went under the water to be baptized.

Then John testified, "I saw the Spirit descending like a dove from heaven, and it remained on him. And I did not recognize him, but the one who sent me to baptize with water said to me, 'The one on whom you see the Spirit descending and remaining, this is the one who baptizes with the Holy Spirit.' I have both seen and testified that this man is the chosen one of God" (John 1:29-34).

As Jesus came up out of the water, John saw the Spirit descend upon Jesus. But it never says that he saw the sky being ripped open by God the Father. He never said that he heard the thunderous voice of God say, "You are my Son, whom I love; with you I am well pleased." No one witnessed those events. No one heard it. No one felt the blast of air as the sky was split so the Father could get to his son. We know it is true. We know that it happened because Jesus gave testimony that it did.

Many of us have had experiences where God has moved heaven and earth to reach us or we know the stories of people who felt God had to rip through the layers that blinded us or the sins that had bound us. Sometimes it happens in a church. Sometimes it happens at a funeral. Possibly it happens in a foxhole but more often than not as we sit crying out to God. We never feel the sky ripping apart. We never see the veil of the material life splitting from top to bottom. We don't realize that God is pulling one side of the heavens apart from another part of the heavens to reach into our lives. We never know it until it happens.

It may have happened to you. You didn't see or feel it. But you know when he reached you. You know when he pulled away the things that blinded you to his love and to his salvation. What God did to reach his son, he is doing for us. God does not want the barriers between us. He wants you in perfect communion with him.

During Lent, we need to use that time to open ourselves to the works of God in our lives. It is a time to draw closer, to feel his presence and to prepare ourselves for that moment when God tears open the heavens and reaches us.

As a pastor, I have been honored to sit with good members of the church as they waited to draw their last breath. The rooms were often somber, some were joyful at the home calling of a beloved one. Some were filled with tears. In every situation, I have never seen the sky tearing open yet that is the exact kind of God we have. He was tearing open the sky to get to my dying friend, to bring that person home to his eternal mansion. God was working. He was tearing the sky. And me, like all the others, we sat unaware. We didn't hear the voice of God. We didn't see or feel the air splitting because that experience was not for us. It was for the saint that laid, drawing their last breath.

As the season of Lent marches on, God is bringing us into a deeper relationship with him. That is if we are seeking it. For too many, Lent begins with a dab of ashes and then hurries toward a basket of candy. Some people may have given up some pleasure as a sign of identifying with Christ's sufferings in the forty days in the wilderness. But Lent is a time when we should be watching the sky. We need to be anticipating the moment when God tears the sky open and reaches deep into our hearts.

God was not finished with his work of tearing. Lent ends at the cross and the resurrection. At the cross there is a wonderful scene that occurs in the temple where the holy of holies is kept. The people were separated from the holy of holies by a thick curtain. The curtain was so heavy it took three hundred priests to carry it. The thickness was that of a man's hand. It was woven like a carpet so it would not tear.

At the end of Christ's journey to the cross, the scripture tells us that when Christ gave up the spirit that this sixty foot high, five inch thick, majestically woven veil was torn. That is the same word as used in today's reading from the gospel of Mark. The veil was torn beginning sixty feet in the air, and ripping down through the entire veil to expose the holy of holies to the people. God was tearing that curtain so he could get to his people and so his people could get to him. Christ's death on the cross was the end of his earthly ministry. To illustrate that Jesus had fulfilled the sacrifice for our sins, the Father tore the curtain that separated him from his people. That tearing was seen by thousands.

These weeks before Good Friday and Easter is a time for you to seek God. He will tear the sky to get to you so you can experience full access to him. On your Lenten journey be looking up for the Father is ripping the sky to bring you closer to him.

Amen.

Second Sunday of Lent
Mark 8:31-38, Mark 9:2-9

Did I Say That Out Loud?

Have you ever been in a situation where you don't know what to say? Many people have. It is hard to imagine that a pastor would ever be in that position. But all of us have faced it, experienced it, and remember that moment. Maybe it was something unbelievable and there you stood with your mouth wide open then suddenly you say something. Yes, you say something incredibly dumb. Been there—done that. Your first thought is often, "Did I say that out loud?" Maybe that was exactly how Peter felt when he, James and John accompanied Jesus into a high mountain six days after the Lord taught a group of disciples that one day he would return in his Father's glory with the holy angels.

Those thoughts most likely ran through Peter, James, and John's minds for the six days. They wondered what his coming in his Father's glory would look like. They most likely questioned if they would be able to take up their crosses and follow him? They may have wondered if they could give up their lives to save the world? Could it be them he was talking about when he said that anyone who gains the world would lose their soul? There were lots of questions in their minds as they climbed the high mountain. The scripture doesn't say that they asked any questions during the climb but don't you wonder what they said to each other during that journey?

As they reached the top, the three disciples would have rested after seeing if their master had any needs. Their love for him and their belief that he was sent from God would have driven them to serve Jesus in any way they could. He needed nothing. Jesus knew exactly why he was there. He was about to be transfigured before their eyes into his glorious form. He was about to stand together with Moses and Elijah. Jesus knew but the three disciples did not. As we know from the Garden of Gethsemane, their desire to be with their master was at times replaced by tired, sleepy bodies. The gospel of Luke says that they were fast asleep. They were not suspecting the glorious sight that would be before them. They had seen miracles but not this. This would have been beyond what they could even imagine.

In the gospel of Luke 9:27, Jesus said, "There are some standing here who will not taste death before they see the kingdom of God." Many may have heard that said and thought that the conquering Messiah would soon come and beat back the Roman army and sit on the throne of Israel. Some may have not understood it all and I am sure that James, John, and Peter did not imagine that they would be the fulfillment of that promise.

Pope Benedict said this about the passage:

"Some—that is to say, the three disciples who accompanied Jesus up the mountain—were promised that they would personally witness the coming of the kingdom of God 'in power.'

On the mountain the three of them saw the glory of God's kingdom shining out of Jesus. On the mountain they were overshadowed by God's holy cloud. On the mountain—in the conversation of the transfigured Jesus with the law and the prophets—they realized that the true Feast of Tabernacles had come. On the mountain they learned that Jesus himself was and is the living Torah, the complete Word of God. On the mountain they saw the 'power' (*dynamis*) of the kingdom that is coming in Christ," (*Jesus of Nazareth*, vol. 1, p. 317).

Can you put yourself in that scene? You are sitting on top of a mountain watching the man you believe to be the Messiah standing on the crest when suddenly he glows. His robe becomes whiter than white and glows. It becomes obvious that what you are seeing is not a hallucination. What appears before you is Jesus in his Father's glory. Then two more figures appear within the glowing light and somehow you recognize that these two men are Moses and Elijah. You would look at the three figures then look at each other. You would be speechless unless, of course, you were Peter - Peter the bold, Peter the leader, Peter the man of action.

Myself, I would have been completely in awe. I would be frozen in the presence of the glory of God. I would not have moved, not said a word, and not made a gesture. Not Peter though. He jumped to his feet and spoke.

As Moses and Elijah were moving to leave, Peter jumped up and said, "Rabbi, it is good for us to be here. Let us put up three shelters—one for you, one for Moses and one for Elijah." At first it appeared that Peter was doing exactly what any of us would do when we don't know what to say. He blurted out something he wished he could take back. But if you examine Luke's account you get a better idea of what he was trying to do. He wanted to prolong this glorious event. He wanted it to be the start of the kingdom of God, right then and there. Because, if this wasn't the start of the kingdom then the things Jesus had said about his death would ultimately come. Peter wanted the kingdom without the cross but the cross had to come before we could all enter the kingdom.

The Transfiguration ended with a cloud descending on them all and the voice of the Father saying he loved his son and that they were to listen to what he said. Soon after they descended the mountain with one question in their minds, "Why did Jesus show them this?" Inside they were absolutely convinced he was the Messiah, the Son of God. There was no longer any doubt. There was no wavering. Not death, or punishment, or banishment would sway their beliefs. Their faith had been strengthened. It was unwavering, that is until the cock crowed three times.

If they had looked within then they would have seen that their presence at the Transfiguration was designed to bolster their faith for the march to the cross. Seeing Jesus for who he truly was and is, always strengthens our faith.

For us today, the Lenten season is a time for us to re-connect to Jesus and his coming in his Father's glory. As we worship together and hear the words of the gospels we start to see Jesus for who he really is. He is the Son of God and nothing will deter his march to the cross and his breaking down the barrier of sin that stands between us, his people, and himself. As I said last week, God is tearing at the sky to get to us. Allow him to get to you.

Amen.

Third Sunday of Lent
John 2:13-22

The Road To The Passover

It was Samuel's twelfth birthday and for the first time in his life, he would accompany his Father Lemuel to the Passover in Jerusalem. Every Jewish male from twelve years on was to make the pilgrimage to the Holy City and to the temple to make their Passover sacrifice. It was a long journey so Lemuel traveled it without his family - until this year. Samuel was twelve and had to accompany his father. He and his father traveled with a caravan of pilgrims for safety. The roads were rough and dusty and the trip was long since most caravans traversed Samaria. Bad blood between the two peoples made Samaria dangerous due to thieves and attacks. Lemuel chose the safest path, mostly because of his son, Samuel.

Along the road, Samuel saw a road sign. It was something that was not needed in his rural area. It said Jerusalem with an arrow. "Are we there, Father?" he asked.

Lemuel laughed. "No, Samuel, that is only a road sign. It points in the direction of the temple. Signs are never the actual thing. Signs help people to find the temple. Signs point the way but they are only signs." Lemuel thought for a moment. He smiled inwardly at the profundity of the thought before he spoke again. "Son, in many ways the temple is also a sign. It points to the day the Messiah will come."

Samuel thought before asking, "When will the Messiah come? I've heard people on pilgrimage talk about a wild man that lives in the wilderness that is baptizing people and he says the kingdom of God is at hand. Some say he might be the Messiah. Do you think we might see him? Do you think he is the Messiah?"

"I've heard the same tales. Most likely they are just that—stories. I've heard that the baptizer does not claim to be the Messiah but a messenger. Some have said he is Elijah who is a forerunner to the Messiah. Scripture tells us that one like Elijah will return to announce the arrival of the Messiah." Lemuel paused before adding, "Honestly, I have only heard tales and they could be nothing but that. Time will tell." The two walked on with Samuel storing up all the comments and the conversation in his heart.

The day and time had come and Samuel's eyes grew wide as he stared at the thousands and thousands of people crammed into the streets of Jerusalem. They were from all over. He heard different languages and saw different clothing. He also saw the Roman soldiers posted along the streets that moved the thick crowd toward the temple. He knew they were there to strike down any rebellion and to keep the faithful from growing unruly. He was afraid to stare at them but couldn't keep from throwing quick, furtive glances in their direction.

Samuel's group pressed on through the city until the temple loomed high before them. The entire area for the temple was about fourteen acres. It was massive therefore thousands could easily join the celebration of the Passover. Thousands were pushing their way into the temple that day.

Far above them, Samuel saw two men standing and talking on a balcony. He looked up. One was dressed in the robes of a priest but not just a simple priest. His adornments and rich fabric clothing made him one of the highest in the priestly line. The other wore the clothing of a Roman leader. The man walking next to Samuel noticed the boy staring at the two men. He nudged him and spoke.

"Boy, that is the high priest Caiaphas. The other is the Roman pig sent to rule over us. He is Pontius Pilate. They both are making money off us poor Jews. The two are thick as thieves."

Samuel was surprised that someone would call a priest a thief. The high priest was the leading teacher, the highest religious figure in the city and at the temple. At the same time he wondered what his walking partner meant. He would soon discover why Caiaphas was believed to be corrupt. Samuel and his father walked on and the temple grew continuously larger in the boy's eyes. The people around him grew thicker as they all approached the gates. The gates were wide to allow people to enter but the throng of pilgrims was greater. The bottleneck slowed each approaching person.

Later Samuel's would know that his walking neighbor was right. When Pilate forced the Roman deity of Caesar upon the Jews, Caiaphas stood back and allowed it. It was Caiaphas who permitted the Court of the Gentiles in the temple to be used for the selling of sacrificial animals, the money changers, and the tax collectors to operate inside the gates. He took his cut from every coin changed and every sacrifice sold. He was defiling the temple to fill his pockets to the tune of millions each year and Pilate took his cut from Caiaphas. They were thick as thieves because they were thieves.

Samuel's eyes grew wider as he strolled into the Court of the Gentiles where it was intended for non-Jews to come and worship. It would be impossible for anyone to worship in the din of noise and the bustling marketplace. His ears rang with the sound of clanking coins piling higher and higher on makeshift wooden tables, cooing doves, the bleating of lambs, and mooing of cattle. He tugged at his father's robe and asked, "Father, why are there so many men sitting at tables changing coins?" They seemed to fill in every possible nook and cranny in what appeared to be the largest marketplace in the land.

Lemuel answered honestly but with a scowl, "Son, the temple tax has to be paid in shekels. Those men are changing our Roman coins into shekels so we can pay our tax. The Roman coins are covered in the images of Caesar that are seen as unclean. Romans consider Caesar a god and we, Jews, only worship one God. Our coins, shekels, carry only non-human images."

"How do we know they are fair when they exchange the coins?"

"They aren't. These are not honest men. They are men here to make money off of us poor pilgrims." Lemuel paused and sighed, "But, son, we have no choice. This the way it is. We accept it so we can have our Passover in Jerusalem as God commanded," Lemuel answered.

The boy stood staring at the pens of animals all around him. "Father, our lambs are more perfect than these. Why did we have to buy one here for the sacrifice? We could have brought one of our own."

"The priests reject animals brought from our villages. The only ones accepted, imperfect or not, are bought here. Again, that is just the way it is. We have no choice." The father turned his son's face toward himself and said, "We didn't come here to change things. We came here to celebrate the Passover. We keep ourselves out of the priest's business and out of Rome's business," his father explained as he approached a money changer. He attempted to negotiate the exchange but he knew it would be fruitless but Lemuel had to try. He and his son walked towards a pen of lambs. It was a makeshift combination of sticks and twine. They looked over the animals. Although, Lemuel knew that two turtle doves would cost him roughly 800% of their real value, he chose to sacrifice a lamb this year since it was the first time Samuel had made the trip.

As he looked over the animals, he shook his head. Samuel was right, any one of their own lambs were better than these. But as he explained to his son, they had no choice. This was how it was to be and he accepted it. He turned to his son and said, "Come, we must finish our ritual cleansing in the *mikveh* pools then we will buy our sacrifice and prepare for our Passover feast."

Before the Passover, a pilgrim must go through a ritual cleansing to bring themselves into a spiritual state. Pools of water were dug in the rock then lined with plaster. Those who were to take part in the feast needed to clean themselves first. The cleansing would usually take seven days and often began on the pilgrimage.

For each of us, in the service today, our Lenten season is meant to be a time when we take forty days to spiritually prepare ourselves for Easter much like Jesus took forty days in the wilderness to prepare himself for his ministry. Spiritual preparation before a religious day is a centuries old tradition. Jesus followed those same traditions. The pilgrims followed those same traditions and at this present time, you, too, are following the tradition of spiritual preparation. We are preparing by cleansing our own temples, our bodies, our lives and our minds. We are preparing to meet the living Christ on Easter day. Samuel's story will be clearer to us if we keep this age old tradition of cleansing in our minds.

Samuel and Lemuel prepared themselves in the *mikveh* (mick-va) pool. Once they were cleansed, the two walked back toward the fenced-in lambs but Samuel was distracted. People were running from the temple porches into the dirty courtyard. Behind them were lambs racing to freedom, their bleating was loud. He saw doves rising into the air. The sound of wooden tables crashing to the ground followed by the clanging of coins being strewn across the stone porches reached his ear only a moment before he saw the figure of a man ripping open the pens, releasing more animals then tossing a table filled with coins to the earth. The strong figure carried a whip made from cords that he cracked in the air above the cattle. The man's eyes were bright but had a sadness to them.

If John the Baptist was the forerunner to the Messiah, then is this the one prophesied about in the scripture? He watched closely.

Jesus broke open a cage of doves and scattered them while pointing his finger at the sellers. He commanded them, "Get these out of here! You are turning my Father's house into a market!" Jesus pushed over another table of coins before taking another step. He was now directly in front of Samuel. The boy stared at his face.

Before Jesus could take another step, the Jews and the merchants inside the Court of the Gentiles shouted angrily toward him, "What sign or miracles can you show us to prove your authority to do all this?" Samuel stared at this man others called Jesus. If he was the Messiah would he do a miracle in front of them? Was he there to free the nation of Israel? Samuel waited for the reply.

Jesus answered them, "Destroy this temple, and I will raise it again in three days."

The Jews were taken back. Some laughed. Some grew angry that this mad man would interrupt their money making and then say something as preposterous at that. They replied, "It has taken 46 years to build this temple, and you are going to raise it in three days?"

Jesus pushed his way past the Jews and toward the gate.

Samuel didn't understand what he had meant by the temple. He looked around him at the great structure and he could not understand how one man could build it again in three days. He thought long and hard over the next few days as they finished the Passover Celebration and began their journey back home. He listened to learned men discuss what they had seen and heard. They discussed the scripture and the words sunk deep into his mind.

Over the next two years, the father and son traveled to the Passover in Jerusalem. Samuel caught glimpses of Jesus as he strode through the Court of the Gentiles. He had heard stories of great miracles conducted by this young rabbi. He had seen nothing himself but Samuel had heard of the miracles and he heard people talk. Some believed. Others said they had been there when he fed five thousand people from a few loaves of bread and a couple fish. Others were frightened that Jesus would bring the Roman occupiers down on their heads by rhetoric.

Three years after Samuel and his father had gone to their first Passover together, Lemuel fell sick. He was unable to make the journey and Samuel was needed to tend to family business and watch over his mother and three sisters. The week was moving slowly in his small village. He was helping his sisters bring water from the well, when a traveler came through telling the news that Pontius Pilate and Caiaphas had condemned Jesus and He was crucified on a cross. Samuel's heart sank but he noticed a glint of joy in the traveler's eyes. The man went on to say, "But three days later Jesus rose from the dead." The traveler said that he saw the empty tomb himself. It was a miracle.

Three days, Samuel thought, "In three days Jesus would raise the temple. Samuel thought hard about his encounter with Jesus. Then it struck him that Jesus said that he was the temple that would be raised again in three days. He could see plainly that the temple Samuel had stood in was like a road sign pointing to the Messiah. He understood then that this Jesus that had stood so close to him in the temple three years before was actually the Messiah. At that moment he believed that Jesus was the Son of God, who like the lamb Samuel and his father had sacrificed, was sacrificed for the sins of the world.

As we reflect during our Lenten journey, we need to store up the things we will hear and have heard about Jesus. We need to continue to make our journey of spiritual cleansing as we approach Good Friday and then the Lord's marvelous resurrection on Easter Sunday. May Samuel's story help us to prepare for that wonderful day.

   Amen.

Fourth Sunday of Lent
John 3:14-21

A Nod Of Recognition

There was a game show on television. Some of you may remember the 1970's remake of it, and a few may even remember the original from the early 1950's. It was one of those shows that keeps cycling back into our lives in different formats. Today, iTunes even has a version of the game. It is called "Name That Tune." The rules were simple, the host would play a few notes from a popular song and the contestants tried to be the first to guess it. There are some songs that are easy to recognize from the first note and others that elude our memories up until that first word of the song.

Many of us do not have that kind of recall but there must be an equal amount of people that hear that first note on the radio and quickly turn up the volume because they know what is coming. Or they may switch the station to something else. This type of recall comes from the months of hearing it on the radio, on an iPod, or on a CD.

We learn many things through our ears. If we hear old Uncle Bill's stories long enough, over enough years, we remember the stories and the details to a point where we can repeat them along with him. The oral teaching method works the same way. It was used in the time of Jesus when preparing young students to be rabbis and teachers. The mention of a line or the theme from a biblical passage would call to mind the entire passage, the teachings on it and the meaning. Jesus often used this method when dealing with the religious leaders of his day. In our gospel reading today, we covered well known verses. One of them, John 3:16, may have been the first verse you ever memorized, except for the shortest verse in the Bible, "Jesus wept." We've heard John 3:16 enough that we understand that it is the gospel message in miniature. But do we know the context, the story behind it and how Jesus taught Nicodemus, an aged Pharisee the truth of his coming?

It was after dark when Nicodemus found Jesus away from his disciples. Nicodemus traveled after the sun had gone down so he would not be detected. He had not gone on official business. He had not gone to test Jesus. He was there because he had questions. He knew the scriptures and what Jesus was saying in public was not against the teachings of the scriptures. In fact, his words brought new light to the passages. Nicodemus was inquisitive but he was cautious. If other Pharisees and religious leaders found out he had met with Jesus, there would have been a shadow on his own reputation. As the old saying goes, "Lie down with dogs and you come up with fleas." So, Nicodemus was cautious and came at night in the cover of darkness.

The two had barely gotten into their conversation when Jesus threw out a line that would draw Nicodemus' mind back to a great scriptural story. Jesus said, "Just as Moses lifted up the snake in the wilderness." Much like in the game "Name That Tune," the moment Jesus said that the entire story would have rushed through Nicodemus' mind.

In the book of Numbers 21:4-9, it reads, "They traveled from Mount Hor along the route to the Red Sea, to go around Edom. But the people grew impatient on the way; they spoke against God and against Moses, and said, "Why have you brought us up out of Egypt to die in the wilderness? There is no bread! There is no water! And we detest this miserable food!"

Then the Lord sent venomous snakes among them; they bit the people and many Israelites died. The people came to

Moses and said, "We sinned when we spoke against the Lord and against you. Pray that the Lord will take the snakes away from us." Moses prayed for the people.

The Lord said to Moses, "Make a snake and put it up on a pole; anyone who is bitten can look at it and live." Moses made a bronze snake and put it up on a pole. Then when anyone was bitten by a snake and looked at the bronze snake, they lived."

Nicodemus's would have remembered this story. He would have pictured the bronze snake on the pole. He would have known the context of the passage, that the Jews were once again in rebellion against God. They complained once again that Moses had taken them out of their pleasant, peaceful life as slaves in abject poverty with little to eat and little to live for just for them to die in the desert. It amazes me and others how much the wandering Jews romanticized their lives in Egypt. They often wished to go back.

In the early 1980's Keith Green became one of the leaders of the Christian rock movement. One of his classic songs was a parody of this desire to go back to Egypt. It was entitled "So You Wanna Go Back To Egypt." It is worth a listen on YouTube and will help you understand the insanity of their wishes in a humorous light.

One of the best images Keith Green conjures up is about manna: eating manna morning, noon, and night. You should look up the lyrics. They are very catchy.

Nicodemus would have understood this story and the symbol for it was plain that the Savior was the serpent lifted up. It may have shocked the old rabbi that Jesus claimed his deity then explained very simply why he had come into this world in human form. He told Nicodemus that the Father had sent him to be lifted up so mankind could have eternal life.

Much like that serpent raised by Moses on a post, those who recognized they would die once bitten, had to look at it with belief in their hearts. Nicodemus struggled with this simple explanation. He struggled because he was in darkness.

Some have said that when Jesus illustrated that men do their deeds in the dark, that he was referring to Nicodemus coming at night in the veil of darkness. Although his approach to Jesus was not as the evil religious leaders would intend, it was to mask his approach. He loved his position and the perks that came with it more than the answer he received. When Nicodemus heard he would need a new spiritual birth, he could not conceive it. He was a learned Rabbi, a religious leader of the Jewish people. Wasn't that enough to prove his love for God?

It is the same question many people ask today. I go to church. I serve on a board. I give my tithe. I even visit the sick and the shut-ins. Isn't that enough to prove that I am a believer? No, would be Jesus' answer. It isn't enough until we look upon the Son of Man lifted up on the cross and believe that he was offered up to pay for our sins. At that point your Lenten journey truly begins. For it all heads to that point where Jesus is nailed to cross, dies for us and then is resurrected on Easter. That is what this season is about. Look up at the Son of Man, believe and you will be saved.

Nicodemus continued to argue the point. He really didn't get it at all. Jesus was quite direct. He let Nicodemus know that he couldn't see the spiritual point because he was spiritually dead. Imagine how well that comment went over with Nicodemus. He was a "spiritual" leader of his people. He had studied the scriptures, the law, and all of the Old Testament, most likely twice as long as Jesus, and this young rabbi told the older, learned man that he was in spiritual darkness. He told him that he could not understand the spiritual implications of Jesus' teachings because he was not born of the spirit. In other words, he was still spiritually dead.

It would be like, if you, after a few Bible studies, went to a cardinal or a bishop and told them they were seeing the scriptures wrong and you were going to straighten them out. Why would they believe you? At best they would dismiss you as a nut. At worst, they would argue your points with logic and verses. Nicodemus argued with logic. He wanted to know how he could be born again. He was a little too large to enter back into his mother's womb and be born again. He missed the point. He did not see a need for a new birth. He did not see a need to have a spiritual awakening. He saw it in worldly terms and Jesus was dealing in spiritual reality.

Nicodemus was confusing his position within the synagogue and his religious duties with his spiritual life. He was putting the cart before the horse. He thought that if he did those things that meant he had a spiritual life. Jesus told him, no, you have to be born again spiritually for those things to mean anything. Having a spiritual life first comes before the labors of the faith.

Many historians believe that Nicodemus got the point and was later born again spiritually. Today we are looking at how this message of spiritual rebirth affects your Lenten journey. Are you relying on your position in the church or your service to the church as a substitute for a spiritual rebirth? If so, listen to the words of Jesus. "You must be born again."

Amen.

Fifth Sunday in Lent
John 12:20-33

An Encounter With Jesus

"We Would See Jesus" has been the title of books, songs, and most likely hundreds of sermons. It is a great phrase loaded with dozens of directions that a preacher can go with a sermon. It is a temptation for any preacher to take the phrase where he wants it to go but the truth is that staying inside this story, without leaping in countless directions, is the very best way to teach and understand what is happening. Let's look at this biblical account and try to see the real story as it unfolds.

It begins with a few Greeks approaching Philip to request a meeting with Jesus. They had come to Jerusalem to worship the one true God. They were obvious converts to Judaism. They had traveled many miles for this wonderful opportunity to attend the Passover feast and be a part of this religion they had adopted. They were Gentiles, not of any Jewish descent. The day was Tuesday following what we call Palm Sunday. Being from out of town and pilgrims from a faraway land, they would have been there to see Jesus riding into town on the back of a donkey. They would have heard the cries of "Hosanna, Hosanna, blessed is he who comes in the name of the Lord!" Their minds would have been set afire. Here they were in Jerusalem at the same time as the man people were declaring to be king of the Jews, the Messiah.

Many of us have been in a place when a famous person is present. The common reaction nowadays is to get a selfie taken with that person so you can show all your friends back home and at work. Some of you have those pictures on your phone right now. Some may have them on your walls at home. Our first reaction is to somehow get near them. Then we tell everyone we know, "Hey, I got a selfie with so and so."

I imagine that was part of what drove them to want to meet Jesus. Another part would be their desire to see if he was for real. Was he really the Messiah they had so recently learned about and believed in? Good question. If I was in their shoes, I would want to know as well. They probably spent Monday asking questions of the other Jews to see what they thought. Some would have been followers and some would have been doubters. By then there were stories of Jesus healing the sick, the lame, the blind, and even raising the dead. They would have heard stories of people raised from the dead. Someone may have pointed out and said, "That guy over there is Lazarus. He was in the grave, rotting away when Jesus called him out the grave. Lazarus was as dead and smelly as an old fish, and look — he's walking around as alive as we are!" The hearts and minds of these Greek men would have been excited. They had to see Jesus.

They spent Monday and Tuesday asking questions and finding out the location of this man everyone called the Savior. Then Tuesday the small group gathered the nerve to go to him. They found a disciple on the edge of the group that surrounded Jesus as he sat teaching. In hushed voices, with a little fear, they asked Philip, "We would see Jesus."

Philip had been with Jesus, walking the roads and listening to his teachings for a few years. Philip slipped away to talk to Andrew. He told him Greek men had come to see Jesus. They were not Jews although they were here to worship our one true God and attend the Passover. Andrew heard the message from Philip. The two then approached Jesus to see if the Greeks could meet him. Why the layers of protection? I suppose the disciples were being cautious but most likely it had to do with the men being Greek, although followers of the Jewish God, they were not part of the Jewish race. They weren't sure if Jesus would accept Greeks. Of course, he did accept them.

The men obviously entered into the teaching area. We could call this the beginning of taking the message of salvation to the Gentiles. They wanted to meet Jesus. They wanted to know if he was the king of the Jews. They wanted to know if all the things they had heard of Jesus were true.

The scripture never says what was on the pilgrim's minds, what they wanted to know, or even how they responded to the teachings Jesus laid down before this group of disciples. What we do know is that Jesus could see their hearts. He knew their questions and knew their stumbling blocks. Then Jesus laid out simply what it meant to be a believer and a follower.

A few weeks ago you entered into this year's Lenten journey. Why? Because you, like the Greeks, wanted to see Jesus. You wanted your doubts and your fears washed away. You wanted your sins forgiven and you wanted to meet Jesus in a real way. In many ways, we are just like the Greeks. We have heard of Jesus. We've read stories of Jesus. We've heard sermons about Jesus but all those things had still left questions, possibly doubt, and possibly pain. We needed more of God, more of Christ, and so we took the first step towards seeing Jesus. Our lives before weren't enough. We decided we wanted more than three dollars' worth of God. Wilbur Reese wrote this short, tongue-in-cheek piece.

"I would like to buy three dollars' worth of God, please. Not enough to explode my soul or disturb my sleep, but just enough of him to equal a cup of warm milk or a snooze in the sunshine. I don't want enough of him to make me love a black man or pick beets with a migrant. I want ecstasy, not transformation. I want the warmth of the womb, not a new birth. I want a pound of the eternal in a paper sack, please. I would like to buy three dollars' worth of God, please."

You entered your Lenten journey because you knew that you hadn't given your whole heart to Jesus. You've been buying only three dollars' worth of God, whenever you needed it. When a child was sick you would stop by and buy three dollars' worth. When there were struggles and stress at work, you bought another three dollars' worth. Has it been enough? Listen to what Jesus taught the Greeks and the disciples.

"The hour has come for the Son of Man to be glorified. Very truly I tell you, unless a kernel of wheat falls to the ground and dies, it remains only a single seed. But if it dies, it produces many seeds. Anyone who loves their life will lose it, while anyone who hates their life in this world will keep it for eternal life. Whoever serves me must follow me; and where I am, my servant also will be. My Father will honor the one who serves me."

There comes a time in our journeys when we realize that we must serve Christ in order to follow hm. When we serve God we get a lot more than three dollars' worth of God. We get honor. We get eternal life. This is the point in your spiritual journey when you have to make that decision. Can you exist on a few dollars' worth of God every couple of months? Or do you need to be like that kernel of wheat that falls into the ground and dies to yourself, so that you produce an abundance of seeds?

Amen.

Palm Sunday / Passion Sunday
Mark 11:1-11, John 12:12-16

It's Sunday...But Friday's Comin'

As a pastor and a preacher I've developed my own top ten of messages I've heard preached by other men and women. One of my favorites is Tony Campolo's "Its Friday... But Sunday's Comin.'" Dr. Campolo told the story of a little preaching competition that he had with his pastor during services at the church where he attended. Dr. Campolo told how he preached the perfect sermon, perfect in every way. He had taken the congregation to the heights of glory and the depths of despair. As he sat down beside his pastor, Dr. Campolo patted him on the knee and simply said, "Top that." The older black pastor looked at him and said, "Boy, watch the master."

It was a simple sermon, starting softly; building in volume and intensity until the entire congregation was completely involved, repeating the phrases in unison. The sermon went something like this:

It's Friday. Jesus is arrested in the garden where he was praying. But Sunday's coming.
It's Friday. The disciples are hiding and Peter's denying that he knows the Lord. But Sunday's coming.
It's Friday. Jesus is beaten, mocked, and spit upon. But Sunday's coming.
It's Friday. Those Roman soldiers are flogging our Lord and they press the crown of thorns down

into his brow. But Sunday's coming.

It's Friday. See him walking to Calvary, the blood dripping from His body. See the cross crashing down on his back as he stumbles beneath the load. It's Friday; but Sunday's coming.

It's Friday. See those Roman soldiers driving the nails into the feet and hands of my Lord. Hear my Jesus cry, "Father, forgive them." It's Friday; but Sunday's coming.

It's Friday. Jesus is hanging on the cross, bloody and dying. But Sunday's coming.

It's Friday. Jesus is hanging on the cross, heaven is weeping and hell is partying. But that's because it's Friday, and they don't know it, but Sunday's a coming.

By the end of the message the old preacher was simply calling out, "It's Friday" and the whole congregation was responding, "Sunday's coming!"

You have heard the Palm Sunday story before and maybe you thought like I did that this is the exact opposite of the story of Good Friday. Because this was Sunday, Palm Sunday, and Good Friday's coming.

All the people were waving palms, throwing their cloaks, coats, wraps and Ralph Lauren sweaters on the pathway before Christ. It looked like someone had emptied the Salvation Army shed into the streets. People were cheering, "Hosanna, hosanna. Blessed is he who comes in the name of the Lord!"

The crowds ran to the palm trees and cut fronds from them and laid them before Jesus as he approached on a foal of a donkey. "Yay, Jesus. You're the messiah. Yay, Jesus. We saw you raise the dead. Yay, Jesus. You've come to save us. Hosanna. Hosanna!"

But that was Sunday and Friday's coming.

On Friday that same group of people would stand and

scream, "Crucify him! Crucify him! That same group of people that yelled "Hosanna!" would five days later scream out for his blood. They would scream out that he be nailed to a cross. Does that surprise you? Does that shock you? If you were a disciple like Peter, James, or John or the other nine wouldn't you be surprised, possibly shocked, certainly dismayed, and definitely discouraged?

They shouldn't have been and neither should we because Jesus warned them and Mark recorded it in chapter 4 of his gospel. Jesus was teaching his disciples through parables, which are word pictures designed to teach a point. Mark wrote in 4:3-9:

> *"Listen! A farmer went out to sow his seed. As he was scattering the seed, some fell along the path, and the birds came and ate it up. Some fell on rocky places, where it did not have much soil. It sprang up quickly, because the soil was shallow. But when the sun came up, the plants were scorched, and they withered because they had no root. Other seed fell among thorns, which grew up and choked the plants, so that they did not bear grain. Still other seed fell on good soil. It came up, grew and produced a crop, multiplying thirty, sixty, or even a hundred times." Then Jesus said, "He who has ears to hear, let him hear."*

Jesus warned them that this is the way it would be. He told them who he was. He revealed he was the Messiah, the Christ. He cast out the seed that the Messiah had come. He did miracles to prove it. But some people were like the hard ground in the pathway of a garden. These people were so hard, so calloused, and so bitter to the truth that it would bounce off of them. The seed would lay on the surface waiting for Satan to sweep in and do everything he could to steal it away before it germinated, took root and grew. In the crowd that formed around Jesus' triumphant entry there were Jewish religious leaders, Pharisees, who looked at what was going on, then weaseled their way up to Jesus and said, "Teacher, get your disciples under control!" These men hated him and they knew that if Jesus continued to live he would bring the powers of Rome down on their heads, and with that their comfortable lifestyle, power, and prestige would be gone.

I can envision the Pharisees standing and watching. They knew they had to do something or Jesus would bring destruction on their way of life. You can almost hear Satan whispering in their ears with his venomous, sulfuric scented voice, "It's Sunday…but Friday's coming."

There was another group who stood screaming, "Hosanna, Hosanna!" on Palm Sunday. These were the ones that had watched and listened to Jesus. Some were even there when Jesus called Lazarus from grave. They watched as the stone was rolled away and the dead man came forth from his grave clothes. They may have seen him make dinner for everyone out of five loaves and three fish. A few may have been to the wedding where he turned water into wine. They were shouting with great fervency, "Blessed is he who comes in the name of the Lord!"

These people though were like the seeds that fell among the rocks. They sprouted quickly. They saw a miracle here and miracle there and believed this was what the ministry of Jesus was all about. They jumped on the bandwagon quickly but once the heat of the hot sun, the pressure of the Pharisees, came upon them then they withered. The religious leaders pressed hard upon their congregations. They lobbied, cajoled, and threatened those they were in position to pastor. Yes, on Sunday these folks screamed for Jesus the king and then on Friday they screamed for him to be crucified. Yes, I can almost hear the Pharisees saying to their congregations,

"It's Sunday...But Friday's coming." Yes, on Friday you will not scream out Hosanna. On Friday you will not throw your coats at his feet. On Friday you will scream "crucify him" and they will rip his coat from his bloody back and cast lots to see who gets it. It's Sunday now, Jesus' followers, but on Friday you will do our bidding. It's Sunday but Friday's coming.

There was a third group mixed into the crowd. They ran to the streets stripping off their coats, grabbing palms, and throwing them at Jesus' feet but they were like the seeds that fell among the thorns. The thorns or pressures of life grew up and choked them out. On Sunday they yelled, "Hosanna, hosanna, blessed is he who comes in the name of the Lord!" But that was Sunday.

On Monday, the bills for the new Passover outfits for the kids and that great new bonnet for mom came in the mail. How was he going to pay them all, and the mortgage, and still buy food? Then on Tuesday, a Pharisee priest stopped by and said if they continued to follow this Jesus they would be excommunicated and shunned by their beloved fellowship. They would have no friends. They would have no center to their spiritual and social lives. They would be like outcasts. On Wednesday, as the family walked through the marketplace to get the supplies they needed for the Passover meal, they were ridiculed and mocked. They were called Jesus Freaks and people wouldn't wait on them. Finally, by Thursday when the good lady's husband came home early from work and said he had lost his job because his wife was at the Palm Sunday rally yelling out "Hosanna, Hosanna!" she lost her cool. She couldn't take the pressure anymore. She was distraught. When Friday came she was at the front of the crowd teaching her children a new phrase, no longer was she yelling "Hosanna!" but "Crucify him!" I can almost hear the leaders in the community whispering behind the cheering crowds as Jesus rode down the street on the back of a donkey, "It's Sunday…but Friday's coming."

In that crowd there were people who heard the word and it transformed their lives. It not only transformed their lives on Sunday when they sincerely yelled, "Hosanna, hosanna, blessed is he who comes in the name of the Lord." It transformed their lives on Monday, Tuesday, Wednesday, and Thursday. They saw hope and a future. They found relief and salvation in this man who was the Messiah. Then on Friday they saw him judged and tried before Pontius Pilate. On Friday they saw soldiers beat him with a whip and press a crown of thorns into his head until blood rolled like tiny rivers down his face. On Friday they saw him carry his heavy cross through town and up a hill known as Golgotha or the Skull. On Friday they saw soldiers rip his bloody garment from his body and cast lots for it. On Friday they watched as he was nailed to a cross. On Friday they watched him die a cruel death. On Friday their lives had been ruined. On Friday their faith had been stripped away from them. On Friday their trust and belief was rocked as they watched him placed into a tomb. On Friday they wept great, bitter tears as the stone was rolled in front of it.

Yes, they were crushed on Friday. Hope was lost on Friday. Everything they screamed for on Palm Sunday was true but now their faith was pierced by the three nails and dashed on the sharp edges of his stony grave. On Palm Sunday they believed he was the Lord. On Palm Sunday they believed he came in the name of the Lord. On Palm Sunday they believed he was the Messiah. On Palm Sunday they believed everything they yelled as they cast palms at his feet. On Palm Sunday they believed it all as they stripped off their coats and threw them down for him to cross. But that was Sunday. Now, Friday had come and on Friday it seemed as if it had all ended. Hope was lost.

They stood around in dark rooms and hidden alleys talking and listening to one another ask, "Were you there when they crucified my Lord?" Another would ask, "Were you there when they nailed him to the cross?" Another would ask through a tear soaked voice, "Were you there when they laid him in the tomb?" Yes, that was Friday. On Friday it seemed as if it were all finished.

Then like the soft wind or was it a gentle breeze, a voice, somewhere from the sky or maybe from the corner or maybe from within, but it was a voice. A voice as powerful and as soothing as if it came from God himself. It was as if the voice of God whispered—

"It's Friday…but Sunday's coming."

Amen.

Maundy Thursday
John 13:1-17, 31b-35

Wash All Of Me

"Pride is concerned with who is right. Humility is concerned with *what* is right." This anonymous quote cuts to the center of our Maundy Thursday lesson. Jesus had been teaching the disciples about humility inside the kingdom of God. That was a lesson they had struggled with. After all their time together, you may remember, the brothers James and John had come to him and asked that Jesus do for them whatever they requested. Let's look at that passage.

> *Then James and John, the sons of Zebedee, came to him. "Teacher," they said, "we want you to do for us whatever we ask."*
> *"What do you want me to do for you?" he asked.*
> *They replied, "Let one of us sit at your right and the other at your left in your glory."*
> *"You don't know what you are asking," Jesus said. "Can you drink the cup I drink or be baptized with the baptism I am baptized with?"*
> *"We can," they answered.*
> *Jesus said to them, "You will drink the cup I drink and be baptized with the baptism I am baptized with, but to sit at my right or left is not for me to grant. These places belong to those for whom they have been prepared."*

When the ten heard about this, they became indignant with James and John. Jesus called them together and said,

"You know that those who are regarded as rulers of the Gentiles lord it over them, and their high officials exercise authority over them. Not so with you. Instead, whoever wants to become great among you must be your servant, and whoever wants to be first must be slave of all. For even the Son of Man did not come to be served, but to serve, and to give his life as a ransom for many."

As we go through the gospels, we can see a pattern of Christ's teaching methods. He would instruct and then later he would use a physical situation to illustrate the point. The Passover meal, or the Last Supper, as we call it, had numerous physical lessons but the one we are dealing with today is the humility of a servant.

This would be a lesson they understood because the washing of the feet of a guest was done by the lowliest of all the slaves or servants in a house. A visitor would have walked all day in the dirty, sandy streets of Jerusalem and their feet would be dirty. It was a common practice for them to be washed just out of common courtesy. Jesus pulled up the basin of water and towels and began to wash their feet. Why? Because it had to be done, and if you notice not one of them was willing to do it for each other. They were all struggling with who would sit on his right and on his left. This was their struggle. It was the struggle of pride, and pride is about self-glory.

In the church world, it is much the same. Some people seek positions of leadership so they can serve the church. Others seek positions so they can lord it over others. Some people strive to serve others. Some people strive to serve traditions. More churches have divided over the color of new carpet than over theological issues because those are the power plays of the prideful. That is seeking to sit at the right hand and left hand, not of Christ, but over the church of gathered Christians. Jesus said that is not the way it should be. The way of the kingdom was to humble yourself and serve one another. Jesus had told them but now he showed them.

The meal was already underway, the scripture tells us, and Judas had already made an excuse as to why he had to leave. Jesus arose from the table, stripped off his outer garments and wrapped a towel around himself. He filled the basin of water and went from disciple to disciple. The scripture doesn't record any protest from the other disciples but it does from Peter. We should be glad he did because Christ's response to Peter's refusal gave us the poignant point of Jesus' lesson.

Peter told Jesus that it was not the master who should be washing the servants' feet but the servant should be washing the master's feet. This was a true argument for that time in history. What Peter confused was the action for the message within it. I suppose they all missed the message. Peter's response gave Jesus the opportunity to teach.

The first thing Jesus taught was that we need to obey. Jesus said, "Unless I wash you, you have no part with me." Peter could not refuse to do as his master wished. To refuse was to be disobedient to Jesus' wishes. Peter understood that point quickly and said Jesus could wash all of him. It was his statement that he was giving his all to Jesus.

In Christ's response there is a key to what has already transpired in the lives of the disciples. They were already clean - except for one. That would be Judas. Jesus said, "Those who have had a bath need only to wash their feet; their whole body is clean. And you are clean, though not every one of you." He knew who was going to betray him, and that was why he said not everyone was clean."

How would Jesus know that one was unclean? Had he followed Judas? Had he had him followed? The simplest answer is that Jesus already knew that one would betray him.

It was prophesied that one would betray him. Also, because God sees our hearts, Christ knew that Judas had not been spiritually cleansed. On the other hand, he knew the other eleven disciples had been born of the spirit , as Jesus had told Nicodemus.

Thirdly, Jesus wanted them to see the physical act in a spiritual light. He wanted his disciples to see the act of doing the slave's job of washing feet as a symbol of the way they were to lead the coming church. He wanted them to see themselves as servants to each other and God. That was his message, so profoundly taught, through taking what they knew, that the lowliest servant washed the feet of the guests, and turning it into the great lesson of the church. We are to serve one another. We are to humble ourselves to the lowliest jobs. We are not to look upon any act of service as being too low for us for being too far outside our position. We are simply to obey.

As Lent draws to a close, it is time to consider how you want to serve God. The best place to begin is by obedience and humility. Put your heart in the right place. Humble yourself to do whatever it is that God calls you to do. Then when he calls—be obedient.

Amen.

Good Friday
John 18:1, 19:42

Get The Picture?

Each one of us is either a mother, a brother, a sister, a father, or a friend to someone. We have all felt the loss when a relationship or a relation passes from this life to the next. We know the pain, the depression and grief of that loss. (*You may wish to insert a personal loss here.*) I know and you know it.

Try to imagine the pain of Mary, Jesus' mother; Peter, his disciple; John, a faithful follower; or even Mary Magdalene, a wretched soul saved by his loving spirit. Can you feel their horror as the hammer came down on that first nail? They heard his cry of anguish and the gasp of the crowd. Then silence as the second nail was snatched from the bucket and the Roman soldier moved to the next hand. The thump came again. Another cry of anguish and another gasp from those watching.

You look over and see the smug faces of the religious leaders. They feigned sadness, concern, or even a distaste for the actions before them but all along they lobbied, pressed, and lied to get this rabble rouser to the cross. Jesus had called them whitewashed tombs. He had pointed out that they had followed the letter of the law but could not recognize the Messiah when he stood in front of them. Yes, they feigned shock, pity, and sorrow but inside each one of the religious leaders was filled with a secret joy, a smugness of religiosity, and a depth of self-righteousness.

The Roman soldier moved to Jesus' feet and crossed them. He was a practiced executioner. He placed his nail in the right place and brought back the hammer. He took pride in being able to drive it through and into the wood in one blow. He swung. The hammer struck the nail with a powerful thump. Jesus cried out in pain again. Those who love him gasped loudly. The colorfully robed Sadducees and Pharisees looked away, not in horror, not in revulsion, but to hide the satisfying smiles that wanted to escape their lips.

The soldiers raised the cross, an exclusively Roman method of torture and death, and dropped it into the hole. His flesh, muscles, and tendons tore as his full weight was now suspended by the large spikes driven into his body.

Do you think the religious leaders recalled Isaiah 53:7 where the prophet said, "He is brought as a lamb to the slaughter…?" Or Isaiah 50:6, "I gave my back to the smiters [scourgers], and my cheeks to them that plucked off the hair; I did not hide my face from shame and spitting?" Or could the words of David in Psalm 22:16, "Dogs have surrounded me; a band of evildoers have encircled me; they have pierced my hands and my feet…" have come to their minds? When the soldiers played dice to see who got his garments did Psalm 22:18, "They divide my garments among them and cast lots upon my vesture," slip from their memories into their thoughts?

Did the disciples remember the many times that Jesus told them that the Son of Man must be lifted up and to die? Did they recall the moment a few days before when Jesus drew them aside and said, "We are going up to Jerusalem, and the Son of Man will be delivered over to the chief priests and the teachers of the law. They will condemn him to death and will hand him over to the Gentiles to be mocked, flogged, and crucified. On the third day he will be raised to life!" (Matthew 20:18-19) They certainly didn't remember his comments or they would have been aware and hopeful of the third day when he would rise from the dead.

Peter was already a shrinking pile of remorse for he insisted he would never deny Jesus, yet he did the night before, three times before the crock crowed. The scripture never says where Peter had out-posted himself during the gruesome events. It does tell us where Mary, his mother, was. She stood and watched each nail. She heard his cries of anguish and felt the pain as only a mother can do. All of you who are mothers know what I mean. I have heard women say that since the moment one of their children was born, a part of their mind is attached to them. Their son or daughter was always occupying some space in their thoughts. There is a mother/child link that is never broken, never severed. If you are a mother listening today, you can understand Mary's internal pain, her sadness, her grief. This was her son, dying before her eyes in the most gruesome of ways, in the most degrading of all manners of death. A death only reserved for the most grievous of criminals. Her son, who had healed the sick, given sight to the blind, cured lepers, and even raised people from the dead. Her son, who at a simple request from his mother's lips had turned water into wine at a wedding. Her beloved son was hanging on a cross, blood dripping from his back and from the crown of thorns on his head. The pain inside of her must have been terrible. As a mother, you alone could know that. Mothers, you know her pain.

 As a woman who had lived a very sinful life, Mary Magdalene had stood watching the events as well. Here was a woman who had experienced forgiveness in a magnificent way. Possibly no other disciple had been so radically changed. She knew the power of God to transform a human heart and yet she had to watch Jesus in a most powerless position. Her faith must have been rocked. As a person who knows the power of God in your own life, you can identify with what she was passing through.

 As a pastor, I have sat with people who have become friends, as their last hours passed before them. I've seen the ravages of cancer take a strong man and turn him into a thin shell of himself. For those that had become my friends, it was not an easy thing to watch, to see, or to experience. You've done the same. You felt the pain of the loss, you've witnessed their approach to death, and you grieved when it finally came. Grandchildren and children have watched as a loved one expired after a painfully long period of slowly dying. You understand. The apostle John stood next to Mary, Christ's mother, steadying her in this moment of anguish while he felt his own tremendous depression and pain.

Others stood there too — some mocking some jeering, some in pain, some just waiting for the afternoon's entertainment to end. To many the death of this man meant little. To others it was a culmination of their wicked plan. To some it seemed like the end of a dream that had turned into a nightmare.

What about you? Can you imagine yourself in that crowd? You've just made a Lenten journey with a hope that your life would change, that your sacrifices would make you a stronger, better Christian, and that you would be drawn deeper and deeper into a relationship with the Savior. How would you be feeling at this moment as you stared upon your Savior hanging before you shedding his blood?

Can you see why he is doing it? Do you realize that he is doing it for all mankind? Do you understand that he is being sacrificed like a lamb at the Passover for the forgiveness of sins? Do you realize he is doing it for me, for the person next to you, for your parents, for your family, for your children? Most of all, do you realize that his death on the cross was for you? Your sins, my sins, all of our sins are the nails that held him to that cross. When he uttered those words, 'It is finished,' he had paid for every sin and now we simply need to accept it. For on the cross it was finished.

Amen.

The Resurrection Of Our Lord / Easter Sunday
John 20:1-18 or Mark 16:1-8

Profiles In Joy

Little Philip, born with Down's syndrome, attended a third-grade Sunday school class with several eight-year-old boys and girls. Typical of that age, the children did not readily accept Philip with his differences, according to an article in *Leadership* magazine. But because of a creative teacher, they began to care about Philip and accept him as part of the group, though not fully. The Sunday after Easter the teacher brought pantyhose containers, the kind that look like large eggs. Each receiving one, the children were told to go outside on that lovely spring day, find some symbol for new life, and put it in the egg-like container. Back in the classroom, they would share their new-life symbols, opening the containers one by one in surprise fashion.

After running about the church property in wild confusion, the students returned to the classroom and placed the containers on the table. Surrounded by the children, the teacher began to open them one by one. After each one, whether flower, butterfly, or leaf, the class would ooh and ahh. Then one was opened, revealing nothing inside. The children exclaimed, "That's stupid. That's not fair. Somebody didn't do their assignment." Philip spoke up, "That's mine."

"Philip, you don't ever do things right!" the student retorted. "There's nothing there!"

"I did so do it," Philip insisted. "I did do it. It's empty. The tomb was empty!" Silence followed. From then on Philip became a full member of the class.

He died not long afterward from an infection most normal children would have shrugged off. At the funeral this class of eight-year-olds marched up to the altar not with flowers, but with their Sunday school teacher, each laid upon it an empty pantyhose egg.

Mary Magdalene and other women rose from restless and sleepless beds, and gathered the ointments they needed to anoint the crucified body of Jesus. He had been hurriedly placed in a borrowed tomb without being anointed for burial. Their plan was to arrive early and perform this task. Their silhouettes moved toward the tomb. I'm sure they carried sorrowful hearts with them. I'm sure that each step toward the beaten and tortured body of Jesus wasn't easy for them to take but it was a job that had to be done.

Not one of them was thinking about the many times Jesus said that he would arise from the dead on the third day. No, there was no mention of that hopeful and joyful moment. Their heavy hearts guided their heavy feet toward a heavy duty through the heavy fog. They had planned to have the soldiers roll away the stone so they could get inside. They didn't feel that the men could deny them this simple ritual. As they approached, something was wrong.

The stone had been rolled away. The women ran the remaining yards and peered inside to see an empty tomb. One would imagine that at that moment, his prophecies of rising from the grave would have been forefront in their minds but they weren't. Mary Magdalene dropped her bundles and ran toward where they knew John and Peter were hiding from the crowds. Her news was simple. It had nothing to do with a resurrection. It only had to do with an empty tomb and the missing body. There was still no recognition in her mind that, as Jesus predicted, that he had risen from the dead.

John and Peter raced from the room they were hiding in. Fear of the high priest, the religious leaders or the scribes wasn't in their hearts. For Peter, who was often driven by his anger, it was probably another indignity that the wretched religious leaders would add insult to their injury. He ran hard but John was faster. John made it to the opening of the tomb and looked in. Peter came second but didn't stop at the gaping hole in the rock. Then John followed him in. They saw no body but they did see the grave clothes that their master had been wrapped in laying neatly on the cold, stone resting place. The two stared. The scripture tells us that John believed but neither understood what this sight truly meant. We just know that John believed a miracle. What, we are not sure but we know simply that he believed.

After the two had left, Mary Magdalene appeared again at the tomb. When she looked into the tomb she saw two men clothed in a glorious white robes through her sobs and tears. One asked her, "Why are you crying?" It was the same question the man standing behind her asked. Mistaking him for the gardener, she begged of him to tell her where they had taken Jesus's body. She was sobbing hard. Her tears were filling her eyes, it was still early dawn and the light was low. She was asking the right question. Where have they taken his body? In another second she would have that answer in the most miraculous way. Jesus called her name. In that moment, in the midst of the greatest of all sorrow and the most intense grief of her life, her emotions transformed into the most astounding joy.

Psalm 30:5 had become an experienced reality for Mary Magdalene. It says, "...Weeping may endure for a night, but joy comes in the morning." For truly her weeping had lasted through the night and during her first trip to the tomb but at that moment, all sorrow, all grief, all pain, all fear, all depression was lifted instantaneously and joy came in the morning.

We all know joy. We know it isn't a constant state of emotion yet we have had wonderful periods of it. Maybe it came at your wedding. Maybe it was with the birth of your children or at the birth of niece or nephew. For a grandparent it is a special joy because you know the season of complete spoiling is coming then you can send them home. Trust me, that is a special joy.

For the Christian it may have been the moment when Jesus became your Savior and you felt your sins washed away in the spring of new life. Maybe it was when you helped another seeker cross from death into eternal life. We have all felt joy. For Mary this must have been an uncontrollable joy. She wanted to grab him, hold him, weep at his feet but at that point Jesus had not gone on to his Father. He cautioned not to hold him. Mary Magdalene was filled with joy.

Jesus later appeared to Peter and the other disciples minus Thomas. You can imagine the fear and remorse in Peter's heart before Christ's appearance. He had denied him three times. He had sworn he did not know Jesus. He had let Jesus down. When called upon to give testimony that Jesus was the Messiah, Peter turned his back, denied he knew him, and walked away. He had compounded sorrow and remorse that was eating at his soul.

Many Christians understand that feeling. There are times when we have turned our backs on our faith or on our Lord. We went along to get along. That could even have been the reason you started on your Lenten journey this year. You know how Peter felt. He had two fears, one that Jesus would not appear to him and the other was that Jesus *would* appear to him.

Suddenly Jesus appeared in the room. At first they thought he was a ghost. Luke 24:41 tells us that disbelief was due to another reason. "And while they still did not believe it because of joy and amazement, he asked them, 'Do you have anything here to eat?'" Their reaction to seeing Jesus was both joy and amazement. He proved he was real with the physical action of eating.

Paul tells us in 1 Corinthians 15:6 that Jesus appeared to 500 followers. He appeared to Thomas. He appeared to many people with one unified reaction—joy!

Joy should be our reaction today as we celebrate Easter morning. The disciples saw Jesus and they were filled with joy. Yet Jesus holds a special blessing for those of us who have experienced his reality, his power, his grace, and his love. John 20:29 says, "Blessed are those who have not seen and yet have believed." The message of the resurrection is a simple one. Jesus came, died, was buried, and then rose from the dead. You either believe without seeing him or you do not.

As Jesus said, "Blessed are those who have not seen and yet have believed."

The Lord is risen!

He has risen indeed.

Amen.

Easter 2
John 20:19-31

I Doubt It!

(This sermon requires previous set-up for the opening. The writer suggests a male member of the congregation is prepared ahead of time to call the pastor on his cell phone. They should follow the script below.)

This morning will be a little different. I am expecting a call from a well-known person. I am taking the call during the service and will put it on speaker phone so everyone can hear. You'll recognize who it is and I am sure it will impress you that I get calls from this high-level person.

(Phone rings. Speaker answers).

Speaker: Hello, I am very excited to get this call.

Caller: I doubt it.

Speaker: No, no, truly. It doesn't happen every day around here. You are very welcome in our church.

Caller: I doubt it.

Speaker: You are a big part of this morning's message.

Caller: I doubt it.

Speaker: I've worked hours and hours on this message.

Caller: I doubt it.

Speaker: Okay then, let me get to a few questions that I am sure our congregation is dying to have you answer.

Caller: I doubt it.

Speaker: On the resurrection topic, since we recently celebrated Easter, were you as excited as the other disciples when you heard that Christ had arose?

Caller: I doubt it.

Speaker: When John and Peter said they saw Jesus were you surprised?

Caller: I doubt it.

Speaker: We are running out of time. I only have so many minutes left on my phone. Let me jump to my last question. What was it like to place your fingers in the holes in his hands?

Caller: I did *not* doubt it!

(Speaker hangs up)

In our gospel reading this morning, we heard about the disciple Thomas, who we nicknamed Doubting Thomas throughout the centuries because of his lack of trust in the veracity of his fellow disciples when they said they saw Jesus. Was that a fair assessment of who Thomas was? Or does his doubt strike a chord inside your heart? Inside of us all is a healthy cynicism that critically looks at stories, news, gossip, grocery store tabloids with a raised eyebrow. Inside each of us is a Doubting Thomas. This may have been why this account was placed into our Bible. It is so we can critically deal with something completely outside the realm of normal life.

We don't doubt Christ's crucifixion. We don't doubt that Jesus walked the earth. Those are certainly within the realm of normal life, at least for that time frame. You don't doubt that he was a great teacher or a charismatic leader. These are easy to accept because they lie inside the normal, average, everyday portions of life. But the things that fall outside of that normal life leave you with a few questions, a few doubts. Over the last year, we've been hearing the term "fake news." We are learning to doubt our news media on the truthfulness of a story and the bias behind it. We are growing into cynics, into Doubting Thomas-like characters.

Yet, this really isn't fair to Thomas. Though we know little about him, that little tells us a lot about his character. He was nicknamed "the twin" but the scripture never says who his twin brother was. We also know he was brave and loyal to Jesus. In John 11:16, "So Thomas, called the Twin, said to his fellow disciples, "Let us also go, that we may die with him." A person does not commit themselves to that sort of future unless they are loyal and truly brave. He obviously believed in his master and also believed that Jesus was the Messiah.

What caused this brave and loyal follower to doubt the statements by his fellow apostles that Jesus was risen from the dead and that they had seen him? Psychologists who have studied doubt tell us that there are various reasons. It could be an emotional reaction to a disappointing event. It is like that old saying goes, "Burn me once — shame on you. Burn me twice - shame on me." For Thomas it could have been his intense reaction to the loss of Jesus. He was willing to die for him and then Jesus died. His faith may have been rocked and Thomas' reaction could have come from that.

Also, depression makes it hard to deal with joyous good news. The scripture never says that Thomas fell into depression but something tells me that all of the disciples were rocked by the event at the cross.

There are lists for the cause of doubt but most, like medical, historical, or sinfulness, do not fit into what we know of Thomas. One writer suggested that Thomas was simply that downer type of personality in the group. You've been in meetings where the whole group is excited about an idea and one lonely soul speaks up and says, "It will never work." That theory doesn't ring true when you examine Thomas' statement in John 11:16. It seems the opposite of that downer thinking. He insisted they all go with Jesus so that if he died, they all died. Not exactly an "up" statement that would lead a charge. Not exactly a statement that would be considered putting an end to a good idea. He was a brave and loyal follower of Christ. His doubting statement seems to come more from his great disappointment. His confession of, "My Lord and my God" reflects more of Thomas' faithfulness than his doubt. I think Thomas is getting a bad rap but without his doubt, we would never know that our doubts are often part of the Christian journey. Jesus did not chastise Thomas for doubting.

When it comes to your doubts, and we all have them from time to time, it is good to know that Jesus doesn't reject you. Amazingly, it is said that most atheists, people who don't believe there is a God, are actually angry at God. It seems strange to be angry at someone you state doesn't exist. Too often we find that people who have passed through a difficult time with the loss of a loved one, consider that God let them down and didn't answer their prayers. If God doesn't answer their prayers then he must not exist.

When you doubt, carry your questions to God. Ask him to show you another perspective. Doubt can at times be the great catalyst that moves us forward. Remember, God is not afraid of your questions.

In the weeks after Easter, after you have sought a deeper relationship with God for forty days, there may be a letdown or a satisfaction that you achieved a goal. That letdown leaves room for doubt. It leaves room for a desire to make a spiritual reversal. This is not the time to be a Doubting Thomas but the time to be the brave, faithful follower that Thomas truly was.

Amen.

Easter 3
Luke 22:36b-48

Don't Fall

After New Year's Day an office worker decided to go on a diet. She did fairly well for about a week then she started to think about her one guilty pleasure. It was a cream filled donut from a certain bakery she passed on the way to work. For years she had stopped there regularly to get coffee and a cream filled donut. Not every day but a few times a week. On this one particular morning, as she was getting dressed, she had a craving for one of the donuts, but at the same time she wanted to be strong. And since she was a Christian woman she decided to pray for the strength to get by.

She was still praying as she got into her car. She prayed, "Lord, I do want a donut but if it is your will that I have one please have a parking spot right in front of the door. If there is one then I know you want me to have a donut."

Later as she walked into the office carrying her box of donuts, a co-worker said. "Louise, I thought you were on a diet?" Louise answered and told her story of her prayer that if God wanted her to have a donut there would be a parking spot right in front of the door.

The co-worker asked, "And was there a spot right in front of the door?"

Louise answered, "Praise the Lord! On my seventh time around the block there was a parking spot open in front of the door."

Yes, that was a humorous story for some of us and probably a true story for a few others but it illustrates what Jesus was talking about to his disciples in our gospel reading today. Before Jesus slipped off to pray he told his disciples to pray so they would not fall into temptation. In fact, he said it twice because they needed to hear it twice. They weren't praying while they waited they were sleeping. The three missed the Lord's time of prayer and they missed his anguished time of speaking with the Father because they were asleep. So, Jesus told them again, "Get up and pray so that you will not fall into temptation."

Looking at this passage you may be tempted to say, "I've tried that and I still felt tempted." True, you may be. You may even be tempted in the midst of your prayer. Temptation comes when we are weakest and when we are strongest. As long as we are in our bodies, in the flesh, we will be tempted. There is nothing new and nothing special about that. So how does prayer keep us from falling into temptation when a temptation hits? We often have no control over the moment we are tempted. Unless you draw away completely from the world and lock yourself away from worldly and fleshly influences you will never avoid temptation.

What Jesus was instructing them to do was to pray in order have the strength not to fall into temptation. Louise's story is the perfect example of this. She was tempted. She prayed. That first time driving past the bakery was just temptation. It was the second, third, fourth, fifth, sixth, and seventh time she passed before she found the opening parking spot that was the "falling into temptation."

From the other gospels, we know that Jesus was praying for about an hour while the disciples slept. Jesus had prophesied that Peter would deny him three times in the hours to come. In Peter's mind, it was a done deal. He would never deny Jesus. He was adamant. But he was wrong. Peter even knew what his temptation would be and still he didn't understand the relationship between prayer and his strength to not fall into temptation. So, when temptation came he was spiritually weak and he fell.

Prayer is a weapon against the fall. Temptation comes from all sides, from all places, and attacks us when we least expect. Jesus was giving them an instruction that they would learn and use for the rest of their lives.

When tempted, how do we deal with it? First Corinthians 10:13 gives a plan that should be followed. It says, "No temptation has overtaken you except what is common to mankind. God is faithful; he will not let you be tempted beyond what you can bear. But when you are tempted, he will also provide a way out so that you can endure it."

According to the apostle Paul we must first realize that temptation is going to come. Even if you put one at bay another will raise its ugly little head. It is common for every one of us. Then know absolutely that God is faithful and will strengthen you. He will not allow the temptation to be so great that you cannot bear it.

God, while strengthening you also provides a way out. When he does, don't hesitate. Run, flee, move on, all while crying out "feet don't fail me now!" Why? Because temptation can be powerful and once you slip then you will slide. So, run, baby, run.

I need to caution you that when we speak of temptation we often think of something vile or physical but each person has those areas that if we fall into it, tremendous damage can be done to our lives and the lives of others. One pastor told his story. He had never fallen into temptation with a woman, wasn't gluttonous, and didn't skim from the church coffers. What he had was explosive anger.

Throughout his childhood and teen years, it was uncontrollable. Once it manifested, it was like trying to put Jello® back into that little box it came out of. The endorphins shot through his body like a drug, and like any drug he would explode easily again and again once the anger was released.

He had ruined different careers, different relationships, and different opportunities by quick anger. Seeing what it was doing to his life, he prayed, and then looked for the ways out. As he examined those moments of embarrassing anger that usually ended in broken objects and cowering loved ones, he found a common thread. First, he did it to control a situation that had gotten out of control. Second, he exploded to hide his impending failure. Thirdly, he exploded out of the frustration of not being perfect.

He knew why and he also knew how to handle it. He had to flee. One of his biggest frustrations was handyman work. He, his brothers, and his cousins, joked that the handyman gene wasn't passed down to their family. For this pastor, every endeavor with a tool led to frustration and frustration led to anger. He told this story.

"I needed to put together a shelf to hold some books. I bought a cheap snap together shelving unit made from hard plastic. I should have known the moment it said, *easy to assemble*, that I was in for a battle. Since I know how frustrating working with tools can be for me. I only had a hammer and a screwdriver available in the house. The shelving unit only required half my tools—the hammer. Hammering, I was pretty good at.

"I allotted myself thirty minutes for this little, quick and easy job. I guess I'll never learn. I placed a leg in the hole and whacked it with my hammer. Nothing happened. The plastic leg was too wide for the hole. I smacked it harder. Nothing happened. I tried another leg with the same result. Reasoning, I extracted that each leg would be exactly the same. It only took me three-quarters of the legs to figure that out. I was getting smarter with old age. Then I tried a different shelf with the exact same results. Now I knew why it was so cheap to purchase.

"Then the thought hit me just before I hit my thumb. I saw myself opening the front door and pitching the whole unit down the stairs, running after it then jumping on top of it until it broke to pieces. The visual was as strong as watching a TV show unfold in my mind. There before me was my old nemesis—anger. I was being tempted. 'Remember how good it feels to break things,' it whispered. 'Go ahead. You really liked to scream and swear and break stuff. Remember that exhilaration?'

"Here I was, after years of victory over my anger, the opportunity to explode was right there before me. I stopped. Set everything down and walked to my office where I started back to work on a sermon about, of all things, temptation. I was being tempted. I could walk away and never put the shelf together, which is another form of surrendering, or I could relax and think it through. God provided the door away from temptation and I ran. I finally got the shelf together, at least, in two pieces. Instead of a five shelf unit, I now have two separate shelves of three and two. God gave me the way out and I took it. It isn't perfect but the more I look at it, the more I see God's provision. Thanks, Lord."

We have spent several weeks working on building our spiritual lives up. It is just about that time when the temptation to go back to who we were grows stronger. To continue to grow, we need to stay close to the vine and flee from the temptations that held us back for so long.

Amen.

Easter 4
John 10:11-18

And That's All I Need To Know

As many Sunday school teachers do, Miss Johnson pulled together her young students so they could prepare to memorize Psalm 23. She approached the pastor wanting to have the students present their memory work to the whole congregation on Sunday morning a month from that date.

Little Bobby was initially excited about the memorization and being able to recite his part before the church. He wanted to invite his grandmother to watch him do it. Unfortunately Bobby froze when it came to memorizing just about anything. He tried and tried. His parents helped him but he just couldn't remember the Psalm. After a month of practice he could not remember any more than "The Lord is my shepherd."

That fateful Sunday arrived. The small class walked single file up to the front of the church. All were smiling except for Bobby. He was petrified. Bobby was the first to recite the psalm before the church but by then his nerves made his entire mind go blank. The teacher crouched down in front of him and held the microphone to his face. Bobby suddenly smiled and said, "The Lord is my shepherd and that's all I need to know."

Truly, little Bobby was right. The Lord is our shepherd and once we understand that relationship to our God, to Jesus, then we have a good operational basis for our faith. In our gospel reading for today, Jesus calls himself the Good

Shepherd. In the group listening to him, everyone would understand that imagery. Once again, Jesus started with something they knew and then moved on to applying a spiritual point to it. It was important that they understood that he was a good shepherd. Why? Because, very simply, there were some bad ones.

A bad shepherd, often termed a hireling, would at times be hired to watch the sheep. When a wild animal, a wolf, or a lion, as in the case of David in the Old Testament, would come along to have themselves a bit of a mutton dinner, the hireling would run. The hireling was hired to protect the sheep but to this bad shepherd that didn't go so far as to go face to face with a wild beast. You could hear them as they ran crying out, "Feet don't fail me now!"

How completely the opposite of this is the shepherd in the Parable of the Lost Sheep that Jesus told in Matthew 18:12-13. "What do you think? If a man owns a hundred sheep, and one of them wanders away, will he not leave the 99 on the hills and go to look for the one that wandered off? And if he finds it, truly I tell you, he is happier about that one sheep than about the 99 that did not wander off." That is how a good shepherd was portrayed.

You may remember the story from 1 Samuel of David's trip to take his brothers food when he saw Goliath taunting the Jewish soldiers. King Saul was shocked when David offered to fight the giant. David's only training had been as a shepherd. What did he know about fighting giants? In his answer we see, once again, the spirit of a good shepherd.

"But David said to Saul, 'Your servant has been keeping his father's sheep. When a lion or a bear came and carried off a sheep from the flock, I went after it, struck it, and rescued the sheep from its mouth. When it turned on me, I seized it by its hair, struck it, and killed it. Your servant has killed both the lion and the bear; this uncircumcised Philistine will be like one of them, because he has defied the armies of the living God. The Lord who rescued me from the paw of the lion and the paw of the bear will rescue me from the hand of this Philistine" (I Samuel 17:34-37).

A good shepherd protects his sheep. The disciples were well acquainted with the role of a shepherd. They also would have remembered the parable of the lost sheep and certainly this story of David was told to them as children. A good shepherd, they would know, protects his sheep.

When Jesus told them he was the Good Shepherd he added that he was the kind of good shepherd that would lay down his life for his sheep. If attacked by a lion or a bear, our good shepherd would not run, not give up protection even if it was a battle to the death.

Jesus was the kind of shepherd who would lay down his life for the sheep. When Jesus told them this truth, the disciples did not understand the prophetic nature of his comments. For at that time Jesus was marching toward the cross to do exactly what the Good Shepherd promised them he would do. He was going to lay down his life for the sheep. There is no sign that any of them understood at that time that Jesus, the Good Shepherd, would offer himself up as the Passover lamb for the forgiveness of our sins. I don't believe they understood that but it was certainly easy to grasp that Jesus promised to be their good shepherd.

Not only does the good shepherd protect his sheep but he also said, "I am the Good Shepherd; I know my sheep and my sheep know me." That is certainly a hard thought to process. Jesus said he knew his sheep. How is that possible? With around eight trillion people in the world, God claims to know me, my thoughts, my hopes, my plans, my pains, and my sorrows.

Instead of looking at this as a wonderful and hopeful thing, we all, at times, feel so insignificant. We don't see how our little bit of service to our Lord, or our prayers or our labors for him amount to much. We don't know if God is aware of our struggles, our loneliness, our grief, or our losses. We don't know. We just don't know.

Yet Jesus told us in no uncertain terms that God knows us, each one of us. In Jeremiah 29:11, the Lord tells us, "For I know the plans I have for you," declares the Lord, "plans to prosper you and not to harm you, plans to give you hope and a future." Not only does the Good Shepherd protect, and know us personally but he does have a plan for our lives. We are not insignificant to God. You matter to God. You belong to his flock.

As Matthew 10:29-31 says, "Are not two sparrows sold for a penny? Yet not one of them will fall to the ground outside your Father's care. And even the very hairs of your head are all numbered. So don't be afraid; you are worth more than many sparrows."

The Good Shepherd knows his sheep down to the numbers of hairs on your head and some of you are making his job easier with your hair loss. He knows when you fall. He knows you.

On the flip side, our scripture reading says that his sheep knew his voice. We have talked a lot about our need to be in a relationship with our lord. We know that Christ laid down his life for his herd. We also know, too, that a good shepherd would leave the flock to search for a lost sheep. Are you one of the lost sheep? Have you wondered away from the herd? Are you struggling to hear his voice? Maybe today is the day that you need wander back toward the Good Shepherd. God will rejoice that his wandering sheep has been found. What assurances do you have? You have God's promises and God always keeps his promises.

Remember, the Lord is my shepherd and that is all I need to know.

Amen.

Easter 5
John 15:1-8

How Does Your Garden Grow?

Our scripture reading from the gospel of John tells of Jesus teaching his disciples about remaining connected to him in order to grow strong in their Christian lives. He used an illustration that people of his day would have understood easily. Grapevines were readily handy and they were most likely grown by most homes as a source of food and drink. The disciples, who were once boys, would have tended to the family's vines and would know experientially the right ways to trim, groom, prune, and train a vine. Once again in teaching the disciples, Jesus made a nod of recognition as the beginning point. Just about all of them would have experience with a grapevine and how to make the greatest and most fruitful harvest.

Many of us don't live in an agrarian society. We don't farm our acres everyday but many of us have had experiences with gardening. We have spent time building up the soil to make it rich in the nutrients it needs to grow flowers or vegetables. Some of us have even tried our hands at grapes. But just about everyone has tried their hands at tomatoes.

We buy those little plants filled with promise of super huge beefsteak tomatoes or juicy little grape tomatoes. We gently place them in our cars, drive slowly and carefully home so nothing spills and no leaf is broken . We want to show the world that we are capable of growing world-class tomatoes.

Next we prepare the soil by digging it up and mixing in fertilizer, and maybe even manure of some sort because we are growing award winning tomatoes. We can almost hear the announcement at the county fair for the largest, sweetest tomato in the county as they call your name. We plant the plants next to tomato stakes because we are going to train them to grow high, broad, and with fruit that bends their boughs.

The results, well, only you can tell what the results were. Either you had such a great harvest that you gave them away or like me, you waited for someone to bring you a bag from their plentiful harvest because your plants failed. As people say, some of us have green thumbs and some of us have black thumbs. I will make no further confessions about my thumbs.

If we apply all that we have learned in planting our gardens to this passage, it is much easier to get the spiritual point of Christ's teaching. Apply your experience to the words and you will gain more from what Jesus has to say. Let's look at this passage from that point of view.

Jesus identified three players in the story. The gardener who was the Father; himself, who was the main branch that comes up out of the ground; and the branches, which are you and me. Let's begin with the gardener, the Father, and his role in the story. The gardener begins by choosing the soil. In the gospel of Mark 4:8, Jesus told the simple story of a farmer that went out to sow seed. The seed on the pathway never germinated. The seed on the rocky ground sprung up and withered in the sun because it had no root system. The seed in the thorns was choked out. Mark 4:8 says, "Still other seed fell on good soil. It came up, grew, and produced a crop, some multiplying thirty, some sixty, some a hundred times." If the gardener wants good growth then he chooses good soil. The grape vine needs good soil so the roots can extend down and out equal to what is seen above the ground. The Father chose good soil expecting it to produce bountiful fruit.

Our faith is set in good ground. It is filled with everything we need to grow good fruit. The second epistle of Peter says, "His divine power has given us everything we need for a godly life through our knowledge of him who called us by his own glory and goodness. Through these he has given us his very great and precious promises, so that through them you may participate in the divine nature, having escaped the corruption in the world caused by evil desires"(2 Peter 1:3-4).

To put it in gardening terms, you are planted in good, rich, dark soil. Everything is there for you to grow. It is into that soil that the Father has planted the vine. The main stalk rising from the ground grows up a wooden stake. The main stalk pulls the nutrients from the soil. No branch can exist without it. No branch can bear fruit without it. If you were to cut it off, then even the healthiest branch would not survive. Every branch must be attached to the vine. Jesus is that vine. Without him, you have no spiritual life. Without him, you will produce no fruit of the spirit.

Remember your tomato plants. Occasionally you would bump a branch and it would bend and break part of the way through. A caring, nurturing person would lift it into place, maybe even put a stick under it to hold it up but in reality, the full strength of the ground's nutrients would never get to the buds or the small, green baby tomatoes. It would die.

As a pastor, I often meet people who are like that half-broken branch. They want to grow but somehow life's missteps brush a rough leg by it and it snaps. It tries to grow and produce fruit but it is fruitless until the gardener makes the correct repairs. In many ways, the season of Lent that we passed through was a time when the gardener, the Father, was mending us and healing us so that we could produce fruit once again.

In other words, we must stay attached to the vine. We need to stay attached to Jesus. Everything we need to produce fruit in our spiritual lives flows out of the vine into the branch. As branches though, we must not think that we will immediately grow big, juicy grapes. The gardener has a lot of work to do. First of all, it takes time for the vine to produce branches that bear fruit. As a branch, remember the branches are you and me; we may not produce fruit for a few years. There are lots of things from our former lives before Christ that may hold us back or stunt our growth.

To use a fishers of men analogy, in the church, we like our fish cleaned, battered, and fried but when Christ sends out his fishers of men, the fish they catch are smelly and fighting the change all the way to shore. When you meet Christ you often have habits or addictions that you have spent years developing and that is what Jesus talked about when he said, "He cuts off every branch in me that bears no fruit."

At first that seems as if he is saying that you are thrown away and condemned. But once again, you have to stay in the story. You have ride with the grape vine analogy. The role of the gardener is to help us to bear fruit. One of the ways the Father does that is by pruning. He prunes from our branch, the little shoots that suck off the life from your spiritual journey. He prunes off the things that are part of your old, dead life and throws them in the fire. Yes, you may be fresh on your spiritual journey. You look around this church building and see a lot happy, growing, thriving, fruitful Christians. But if you were to ask that cleaned, battered, and fried fish if he or she was always like that they you would tell you stories that might curl your toes. We all get pruned by the Father. We may not like it when it happens. We may not want it but once we have made it to the point of seeing the wonderful growth of fruit in our lives and then in others then we can see his grace, mercy, and wisdom.

Finally, Jesus gives us the greater goal as to why we are pruned to be fruitful. He says, "If you remain in me and my words remain in you, ask whatever you wish, and it will be done for you. This is to my Father's glory, that you bear much fruit, showing yourselves to be my disciples."

Now, go and bear fruit.

Amen.

Easter 6
John 15:9-17

Love Is A Verb

Most of you may not remember Art Linkletter on television but he always had a section on his show titled "Kids Say the Darndest Things." There is something so very honest and innocent about their views on the world's toughest subjects. Following Linkletter's example, a group of professionals gathered and asked a group of four- to eight-year-olds "What does love mean?" Here are some of their answers.

"When my grandmother got arthritis, she couldn't bend over and paint her toe nails anymore. So my grandfather does it for her all the time, even when his hands got arthritis too. That's love." Rebecca – age 8.

"Love is when a girl puts on perfume and a boy puts on shaving cologne and they go out and smell each other." Karl – age 5.

"Love is what makes you smile when you're tired." Terri – age 4.

"Love is what's in the room with you at Christmas if you stop opening presents and listen."

Bobby – age 7.

"If you want to learn to love better, you should start with a friend who you hate." Nikka – age 6.

"My Mommy loves me more than anybody. You don't see anyone else kissing me to sleep at night." Clare – age 6.

"Love is when Mommy sees Daddy smelly and sweaty and still says he is handsomer than Robert Redford and Brad Pitt." Chris – age 7.

"I know my older sister loves me because she gives me all her old clothes and has to go out and buy new ones." Lauren – age 4.

"You really shouldn't say 'I love you' unless you mean it. But if you mean it, you should say it a lot. People forget." Jessica – age 8.

Here's one of the best from another source.

Author and lecturer Leo Buscaglia judged a contest to discover the most caring child. This is what he said about the winner. "The winner was a four-year-old child whose next door neighbor was an elderly gentleman who had recently lost his wife. Upon seeing the man cry, the little boy went into the old gentleman's yard, climbed onto his lap, and just sat there. When his Mother asked him what he had said to the neighbor, the little boy said, 'Nothing, I just helped him cry.'"

Many of us have a definition of love. That is: *love*, the noun. But in the gospel reading today Jesus gave a command to do the action verb *love*. We are to *love* one another. Why? I believe there are two reasons. The first is that it is what people outside of the church, outside of Christianity, will see.

The second is because inside the church we are a family and what binds us together is our love for one another. That is how it is supposed to work. Not every group of believers, Christians, or church goers experiences that.

There was a news story that circulated years ago about two dwindling congregations that decided to merge. They did but there was a major problem. One group said the Lord's Prayer with the word *debts*. The other said it with the word *trespasses*. I guess the battle waged and raged over a year's time when the two decided to split. The newspaper described the division as "One congregation went back to its debts and the other went back to its trespasses."

The truth is that in congregations loving each other isn't always the case. Sometimes we fail at following Christ's command to love another. And some congregations just do it. There is one group that exists along the Mississippi River. It isn't large and it isn't small. It is a good size where everyone gets to know one another. Their teaching is excellent and their services are filled with worship but the thing they do best is love another.

Every Sunday the group gathers for lunch after the morning service. It is a time of personal announcements, birthday acknowledgments, and recognition of kids that did something good or great. It is filled with love and lots of food. One might call it a love feast in some aspects. The kids play together afterward, the way kids play. Teenage girls walk and giggle and talk the way kids do. But one thing is present and it makes people smile. It is the love of the people for each other.

They are a loving and giving church. If someone is in a financial bind, this church steps up. One woman retired early from a job at a university and took a part-time position as a Christian school librarian. The school forgot to tell her that they would not be paying her throughout the summer. The church stepped up and filled in the financial gap, simply because they loved her.

The pastor's wife's father had retired from the ministry and moved to be near his grandchildren. He literally brought nothing with him but clothes and books. One week later, he moved into an apartment completely furnished through the gifts of a church that didn't know him but loved his daughter. They believe that love is a verb.

There is a small church in New York state, I mean a small church. Each year they provide Thanksgiving dinner for a few hundred people. They even deliver to anyone in the town that wants it. Volunteers come from every church in town to help out. This is the verb love. It is the act of loving one another.

Why would Jesus tell the disciples on his last night with them that they needed to love another? Why did the apostle Paul say in First Corinthians the "greatest of these is love?" When difficult times come we sometimes need someone to help us cry. When good times come we need to celebrate with people who actually care about our joy.

In his excellent book, *The Mark of a Christian*, Francis Schaeffer writes, "All men bear the image of God. They have value, not because they are redeemed, but because they are God's creation in God's image. Modern man, who has rejected this, has no clue as to who he is, and because of this he can find no real value for himself or for other men. Hence, he downgrades the value of other men and produces the horrible thing we face today — a sick culture in which men treat men as inhuman, as machines. As Christians, however, we know the value of men. *All* men are our neighbors, and we are to love them as ourselves. We are to do this on the basis of creation, even if they are not redeemed, for all men have value because they are made in the image of God. Therefore they are to be loved even at great cost."

Love is a verb. We are to love one another but that doesn't mean that we are to ignore loving even non-believers. That church in New York state that did the Thanksgiving dinner for the town didn't ask to see the baptismal certificate of the people attending. In fact, the posters said that it was a dinner "for people who just want to be with people." It was done because they knew the value of mankind. If mankind was worth Christ dying for then they are worth our nonjudgmental love.

We are now in our sixth Sunday after Easter. One of the greatest lessons that we can extract from our various readings, our Lenten walk with Jesus toward the cross, and his resurrection is that there is no greater love than a man lay down his life for his brother. Look back at where we started

on Ash Wednesday and where we are today in our spiritual lives. You have come a long way but now it is time to put your faith into action. Begin that action by focusing on an action verb. We are to love one another. Are you ready to love one another? The great love journey begins now.
    Amen.

Ascension of the Lord
Luke 24:44-53

Your Mission If You Choose To Accept It

The movies and the TV show, *Mission Impossible*, had a catch phrase that occurred at the very beginning of each story — "Your mission if you choose to accept it." The characters in both mediums receive the impossible task, the tape evaporates in some form, and the team sets out to accomplish it. But they have something already working in their favor. They have training. They have tools and like the Joker said about Batman, "they've got great toys." The voice behind the recording doesn't expect Ethan Hunt to press ahead without his team or without their toys. He expects them to use their powerful tools and they do.

The same goes for each of us. There are times when we face a Mission Impossible task like fixing a leaking toilet or stopping a leak in the tub. No matter the situation, Murphy's Law predicts that whatever can go wrong does. Most of the time the problems arise from us not having the right tools to do the job. Have you ever tried to drive in a nail with a shoe or undo a screw with a butter knife? Most of us know those futile attempts. These are not tools but we try to use them as tools. They are the wrong tools and often lead to the wrong outcome. Why do handy people have a garage or basement filled with tools? The answer is easy. The right tools made for the right job increase the odds of you having the right outcome.

In our Gospel reading today, Jesus tells the hundreds of disciples listening to his voice that they now know what they need to know. He has opened their minds and their understanding about who Jesus is. They understand that he is God. They understand why he came to earth. They understand that his sacrifice on the cross was a full and complete payment for their sins but now they have a mission, if they choose to accept it. Their mission is to witness to what they have seen but that they should wait. Wait for what? A power so great that the impossible mission would most certainly come out in their favor.

Jesus wanted to send them a tool, the right tool for the job. He wanted to send them a power tool. Their job was to be his witnesses. Being a witness was easy. You just told people what you saw and what he said. That seems like an easy task but let me ask this one question. Have you done it? Maybe you've sat with a friend or a neighbor. Maybe the conversation came around to spiritual things and they asked you about church and about your faith. Did you sidestep the issue? Do you think that the mission of telling others about who Jesus is and what He did should be the pastor's job? Were you afraid that your friend would somehow think you were one of those religious fanatics? Those fears are common and those fears are real. The world has changed. We tend to be more cautious when talking about spiritual things. Yet, Jesus' last instruction to his disciples as they saw him ascend into heaven was to go back and witness to what they heard and saw. But they were to wait. Some of us are in that perpetual state of waiting. It is always, "I'll wait. I'll talk about that the next time they ask." We don't know what we are waiting for. Waiting, just waiting but waiting for what?

Jesus promised those disciples something. It was a gift of a promise from the Father. It was something so powerful that it could change the lives of anyone who allowed it. After Christ ascended into heaven, the disciples headed back to Jerusalem to wait for the gift the Father was sending them.

It was on the day we call Pentecost that the gift arrived. The disciples were praying earnestly when they all heard the sky rumble and tongues, of what appeared to be fire, descended upon them and each of them was filled with the Holy Spirit, the promised gift of power that Jesus had told them about.

The New Testament uses that word power often and each time the word power is translated from a Greek word that is the root of our English word dynamite. The disciples didn't receive a soft, easy and gentle power. They received a power so great it could be compared to dynamite. When it happened there was a dynamite-like experience in the lives of those who received it then in the lives of those who heard it.

When the Spirit descended on the disciples they began to speak, there's that witness part Jesus told them about. When they spoke in their native language, the crowds forming around them heard in their own native language. Not one disciple had taken a Rosetta Stone course. Not one disciple had studied a foreign language in high school. In fact, they didn't even speak in a foreign language. The miracle was in the hearing. Each person understood the disciples in their own language. That is the dynamite power of the Holy Spirit. That was then but what about now?

Now, back to us and our conversation with a neighbor or a friend about spiritual things. As Jesus commanded, we are called to simply be a witness. That is to say what we know. That is the human part but you have to keep in mind that at the moment of your conversion, you were given the gift of the Holy Spirit. So, when you begin to speak, it is like you reached into your tool box, and you pulled out the right tool, and it is a power tool. You simply talk. You tell what you know. The Holy Spirit, the power tool, does the heavy lifting. The Spirit blasts opens their eyes like dynamite blasts a hole in thick, hard rock and the people begin to hear what they need to hear.

When you are given the opportunity to tell others about Jesus, don't shrink back from the task. When you open your mouth and begin to speak, trust that the Holy Spirit has already begun the work in your friend's life. What you say may not be eloquent but it will be what they need to hear. Why? Because you have reached into the tool box and pulled out the right tool, the Holy Spirit. The Father is drawing your friend to Him but he wants to use you as the vehicle for His message.

People often get very uptight when a pastor says that we should be witnessing. Maybe you think about people standing on the street corner crying out verses to angry crowds around them. Maybe you've tried to talk to someone who was confrontational, or belligerent or just plain nasty. We take that as a rejection of us but quite honestly it really isn't a rejection of us. It is a rejection of Christ. Some people are angry with God. We are not called to make people walk the aisle to the front like a Billy Graham. That is what he is called to do. We are called to just tell the truth about what we know about God and how he has changed our lives. That is when the power tools come out. The Holy Spirit begins his work and your neighbor or friend starts on their journey.

Back on Ash Wednesday, I invited you to start your spiritual journey. You may have started it with an anger towards God. You may have started it with a heavy heart but through the weeks you learned more and the Holy Spirit worked on your heart until you finally discovered who God is and what Jesus has done for us all. That was your journey.

What Jesus tells his disciples to do is to describe their journey and when they do that, the Holy Spirit empowers their words. People then listen and understand. Once they understand then the Holy Spirit will guide them on a journey much like you took.

As we close the Easter season we are called to tell others what we know of Jesus. It may take a long time before the people we talk to make that first step but then again, I chance to say that it took you a long time as well.

Easter 7
John 17:6-19

As You Sent Me, Then I Send Them

In our gospel reading today, Jesus is praying for his disciples. We find that he is broadening the meaning and scope of the title disciple. It not only included those who surrounded him at that moment, and the many who believed in him but it appears to refer to all those who are beyond the Jews. The passage seems to refer to all believers of that time and the future. In other words, even us.

He prays for our protection from the evil one. That we can all appreciate. He also says that he is sending them as the Father sent him. A little closer to home, Christ is implying that we, you and me, are sent out to do the same things as Jesus. We are being sent to teach others about Christ and what he did and about true worship of the Father. You are sent.

Your first thought is that you are not interested in being a missionary. Although that is part of the sending, that isn't the real thought behind it. The sending is a lot closer to home. Think of all the ways we can teach others about Christ. We have several great Sunday school teachers in the church. More and more Christians are discovering that once a child reaches seventeen, it becomes more difficult to win them to Jesus. The "seven to seventeen window" is what they call that time frame when a heart is still open and drinks in the knowledge of their faith. Therefore, we should look at that window as the most open time in a person's life and then realize that a Sunday school teacher and youth pastor are on the front line of the battle for the hearts and soul of people.

Some people claim they have a calling to teach kids. According to this passage it is not so much a calling as a sending. They are sent to do what Jesus said. He is sending us as the Father sent him.

There are many Christians who have joined small group, home Bible studies. Although there is usually a leader in each study, there is also shared opinion, shared knowledge, and shared insights. It is the average church-goer teaching the other average church-goer. It is doing what we are sent to do - to teach one another.

Others have joined prison ministries and spend their time working with those that need redemption and hope. Others allow their hammers to bang out words as they travel and build homes. It could be the person who sits next to you at work. You see and hear their struggles and speak a word of encouragement. You are getting a sense of their needs and possibly a door will open when you can invite them to your house for a Bible study or just for dinner. God will take the conversation where it needs to go. He's sending you. You just need to wait on him to open the doors.

Parents need to model this in the home. Start teaching your children about Jesus. It doesn't have to be a sit-down family devotional time. That is a wonderful thing but families don't have a central nucleus time together. This kid is in soccer, that one is in basketball, and yet another one is running to some club meeting. It is getting difficult but ask them questions about their Sunday school lesson or about the sermon. Allow an outside teaching source to kick questions and ideas into their minds. Be honest if you don't know the answer. Then go find the answer and give it to them. That is a simple way just to keep the conversation open.

We are sent by Jesus, just as the Father sent him. We are sent to teach others. In many ways, that brings us full circle from that Ash Wednesday so many months ago. We started out needing a renewal in our hearts and minds. God has moved on us to a point where we are maturing Christians.

Now it is time to begin our own mission to help others grow in Christ. He is sending you.

Let me end with a funny story. There were four men in an airplane. There was the pilot. There was a boy scout. There was a preacher (we like to be at the center of every story), and the world's smartest man. He was so smart that every move the current president makes, he has to call the world's smartest man and every president for the last twenty years has called him. In fact, every leader of every country calls him before they make a move. He is the world's smartest man.

Suddenly the door to the cockpit flies open and pilot tells the other three, "I have bad news and I have worse news. The bad news is that the plane is going down. I can't do anything to prevent it. Now for the worse news. There are four of us, and only three parachutes."

The pilot continues, "I have a family that needs me so I am taking one." He grabs a chute, opens the door, and jumps.

The world's smartest man jumps up and says, "I am the world's smartest man. The world can't run without me. Everyone needs me." He grabs a bag and jumps.

As pastors go, this preacher was typical. He wanted to get in his last sermon. He said, "Son, you take the parachute. I have peace with God. I know my Savior and I am willing to sacrifice myself for you."

The boy scout waited patiently for a second, then, rolling his eyes, he said, "Cool it, Reverend The world's smartest man just grabbed my backpack and jumped out the door."

That is a perfect illustration of the world we live in. We have thousands and millions of really smart people jumping out airplanes with nothing but backpacks. And we, the ones Jesus has sent, have the parachutes they need. You are being sent to hand out parachutes to those really smart people that miss the obvious. Christ is sending you to pass out parachutes.

Amen.

www.ingramcontent.com/pod-product-compliance
Lightning Source LLC
LaVergne TN
LVHW051702080426
835511LV00017B/2690